Your birth is a waste at death, unless its legacy archives a positive deed for the betterment of humanity.

BARACK HUSSEIN OBAMA

A MESSENGER FOR WORLD PEACE

SAY WHAT ! ?

Laurus Nobilis Noblesse Oblige Oath

Forging World Peace, Modeling Utopian Politics for the Future

Is it Hyperbolic or Ironic dream?

USE YOUR GAVEL

Michael Olugbile II

Your birth is a waste at death, unless its legacy archives a positive deed for the betterment of humanity.

BARACK HUSSEIN OBAMA

A MESSENGER FOR WORLD PEACE

SAY WHAT ! ?

Laurus Nobilis Noblesse Oblige Oath

Forging World Peace, Modeling Utopian Politics for the Future

Is it Hyperbolic or Ironic dream?

USE YOUR GAVEL

Michael Olugbile II

iUniverse, Inc.
Bloomington

BARACK HUSSEIN OBAMA—A Messenger for World Peace
Laurus Nobilis Noblesse Oblige Oath—Forging World Peace, Modeling Utopian Politics for the Future

iUniverse books may be ordered through booksellers or by contacting:

iUniverse
1663 Liberty Drive
Bloomington, IN 47403
www.iuniverse.com
1-800-Authors (1-800-288-4677)

ISBN: 978-1-4759-5302-2 (sc)
ISBN: 978-1-4759-5331-2 (ebk)

Printed in the United States of America

iUniverse rev. date: 10/15/2012

CONTENTS

Obama's Laurus Nobilis Noblesse Oblige Oath vii
Ode to "Oh Say can you see" ix
Immigrants xi
A dawning of a new chapter in American Presidential history xiii
My Opines for World Peace xv
Dedication xxi
Inspirational Acknowledgment xxiii
Foreword xxvii
Preface xxix

Chapter 1 An Iceberg Spec of North America Immigrant Avalanche 1
Chapter 2 2008 Democratic Primaries to November Presidential Election 13
Chapter 3 As an Atypical American President On Home Front 23
Chapter 4 Barack Hussein Obama as Commander-In-Chief on Foreign Front 35
Chapter 5 Second Term I Pray, solidifies "Change! Yes We Can" with "Audacity of Hope" 51
Chapter 6 Whole World future Immigrants deserve a shot at world peace 59

Chapter 7 World Peace Treaty Every human being ought to sign and subscribe to it 65
Chapter 8 Random Thoughts 77

Divine Hope 89

OBAMA'S LAURUS NOBILIS NOBLESSE OBLIGE OATH

Realism I purpose in the Presidential Oath of office Obama took, gives no preference to the maxim of hyperbolic innuendos and definitely carries no ironic beliefs in my thinking and perception of whom I submit Barack Hussein Obama really is and the legacy he would engrave in the history of American Presidency, beginning from his first tenure ad-infinitum.

When Barack Hussein Obama took that Presidential sacrosanct Oath of the United States of America the first time around in 2009, I had a feeling he was promising the whole wide world that he would exemplify atypical Commander-In-Chief Noblesse Oblige prowess, via "Change! Yes We Can" as he backs up his bravery with "Audacity of Hope" from the Oval Office.

Although his Noblesse oblige as in his humble portrayal of his birth, showing he was not born with silver spoon in his mouth as from a rich background, I contend that he has undisputable highborn attribute of moral obligation to display honorable and charitable conduct of nobility obliges.

He barely took office as the forty-fourth President of the United States of America before he was crowned a peace Nobel Laureate. Laurel mark of honor in deed. Like Laurels nobles of Europe, on whom small wreath of Laurel foliage placement, signify victory emblem or distinction of those from whom character display of nobleness in mind and spirit cum exalted moral excellence is civism mandate.

That is the picture I paint of Barack Hussein Obama on the canvas pages of this book, as I envisioned him when he took that sacred Oath of Office to exemplify Laurus Nobilis Noblesse Obliges in his presidency.

When it comes to the sagacious exemplification he has displayed during the first term of his presidency so far, I can only hope that his second term will paint acumen that would show more acute mental discernment and keen practical sense in not only bringing America back from the brink of economic collapse that could have caused world's economic meltdown, but someone who gives the Americans and the whole world in general the exquisite "Audacity of Hope" via "Change! Yes We Can" and I think yes we will sail victorious as long as fate and right thinking faculty of American voters give him the courage of a second term, to hold the helm and row the boat to a peaceful and safe shore.

ODE TO "OH SAY CAN YOU SEE"

ALL RAINBOW COLORS
AND LANGUAGES IN ONE

America harvests from sea to shinning sea
Oh yes! It's true about her colorful **Immigrants**
She boasts of endless land of opportunities
Milk and Honey drip in abundance
Just beware of bumblebees and wasps
You'll command bravery for inheritance

America can and will not be exhausted
Sacrifice gives no preference to end of chivalrous charity
Capitalism prevails as 24/7 maxim
Survival of the fittest is the motto
Impossible mission achieved out of boldness
All she claims with scrupulous valiancy

America the Beautiful Entity of all migrations
"By the people, for the people, to the people"
the world craves
Souls and precious blood shed for freedom
Demands the world becomes a peaceful place
Creator not angry with your soil, you know it
Your calamities induce unflinching faith in God

"Free at last! Free at last" echoes the pastor's distant past
Creator Amen—my son's pigment adjudged harmonious
Brave contents of his heart orates Change! Yes We Can
Status quo of utopian political caliber ejaculates
Audacity of Hope
Horizon Promised Land beckons world Immigrants
All we are saying—Worldly Peace no more
on mountain top

"IN GOD WE TRUST" your canopy for fortress

IMMIGRANTS

If you have left the Garden of Eden via your ancestors, you are an Immigrant wherever you are on planet earth.

Irrespective of ancestral culture, skin color, religion, dialect or ethnicity, America's populace is composed of 5 compound groups of Immigrants.

1. The American Red Indians
2. The Explorers
3. The African Slaves
4. The Legal or Illegal Aliens
5. The extended Offspring of all 4 groups above

MY PITIFUL HEART BLEEDS

I wish I have a way besides this book to tell and show the world, that anyone who hates America directly or otherwise contingent in behavioral exemplification hates him or herself. We are all Immigrants from all over the world, starting from the first Red Indian settlers to the extended Offspring of all the other three Immigrant groups. America is representative of all nationalities, cultures, ethnicities, languages and multi-hues of all human skin colors. Check out a ripe peach fruit, you'll find your skin color somewhere on it. When you peel it off, you'll see fat tissues, then pink flesh, after which your common bone structure as featured in every world Immigrants stares you down, wherever you claim habitat on planet Earth. Obama said "we are all in it together."

TO CLAIM AMERICA YOURS, YOU MUST IDENTIFY WITH ONE OF THE GROUPS, OR BID OPPORTUNITY FOR AMERICAN PRESIDENCY ADIOS.

PRESIDENT BARACK HUSSEIN OBAMA IS A PROOF THAT ANY OFFSPRING OF ALL AMERICA'S IMMIGRANTS CAN LIVE IN THE WHITE HOUSE AS THE COMMANDER-IN-CHIEF BY FATE SOMEDAY.

A DAWNING OF A NEW CHAPTER IN AMERICAN PRESIDENTIAL HISTORY

PRESIDENT GEORGE WASHINTON

President Washington was Number 1 lighter skin pigment who made American Presidency historical and followed by many more like him as in light skin color, as many as from numbers 2 to 43, until the forty-fourth number refreshed history and put a darker skin pigment in the Oval Office of the White House to help reshape America and to forge world peace.

President Obama paves way and models noblesse oblige type of American Presidency, which will once again elevate the United States of America, a nation of reckoning for all others to emulate rather than hate. America is a boiling pot in which Immigrants from around the world sizzle, exhaling aroma of patriotic citizenry, beckoning harmony her constitution hopes for with unflinching courage.

PRESIDENT BARACK OBAMA

"CHANGE, YES WE CAN"
WITH
"AUDACITY OF HOPE"

PRAISE GOD ALMIGHTY. AMEN

MY OPINES FOR WORLD PEACE

Peaceful world is Adam and Eve descendants' dream in silence from time immemorial, but heart craving in prayers, hopes and wishes to come true. Since Y2K didn't welcome Jesus Christ that could bring peace to mankind as several Christian religious preachers made me believe over the years, I contend that there are 3 major problems which make our world not peaceful but chaotic and continue to make peace illusive in our world. These are Religious conflicts, racial disharmony that gave birth to the third problem as in KKK culture of sporadic hanging of fellow human beings, borne out of hate due to difference in skin pigments. All three together constitute the wall making world peace unattainable.

Ironically, I think that Barack Hussein Obama is born a peacemaker and keeper. Why? In my spirituality, I believe that he is gifted with those three major world problems as weapons to help stop what is making world peace mental illusion and denying mankind its attainment. Three attributes the world ought to capitalize on, in manifesting total forgiveness and aim at a peaceful world, are spiritually and naturally embed in President Obama's passage to life as staff for peacekeeping assignment, like Moses used to free the Israelites from the bondage of Pharaoh. "If the various races, nationalities, and ethnic groups who are creating chaos and fomenting warfare with their enemies could be brought to forgive-to forgive totally-themselves, their tragic histories. The injustices that they have suffered in the past, and the hatreds that have hardened into virtual idolatries, we could be on the way to a more peaceful world." (1)

Succinctly, the world is suffering from three immemorial universal problems, which are making world peace impossible. Imagine if the Jews or Christians are not hated by their fellow Arab Muslims in the Middle East, or very light skinned Prince Harry of Great Britain saying "I DO" if he marries the daughter of an African dark skinned King who would be an African Princess, without raising surprising eye brows of his grandmother Her Royal Majesty Queen Elizabeth II of Great Britain, or people stop hanging each other because of the beautiful colors of their skin, I submit that the world will be a little more peaceful.

Irrespective of our differences in believes on how the world was created, a person's spirit should implore the self to respect the difference in theological orthodox way another person views world's creation came into existence. Thereby, practicing one's religion without being judgmentally antagonized for difference in opinion on how world's creation came to pass, mankind could have a chance at world peace. Global crisis need not be so difficult to understand and rectify if the world is peaceful in which case, it will be natural for people to be selfless in giving helping hands to fellow world Immigrants wherever needed, regardless of different religious convictions or multi radiant hues of different colors with which we are all blessed at birth.

It's supposed to be magical the way the sun creates photosynthesis, which feeds the plants with abundant chlorophyll. Magical because if God only physically molded Adam in His own image with mud, and saw that Adam needed a comforter by taking part of Adam's rib to invent Eve, I spiritually submit that we are all distant relatives' descendants of Adam and Eve. Has anyone ever seen a real BLACK or WHITE human being roaming around in this world? Say so or like the rest of us, you are guilty of name calling and detrimental figure of speech crimes. In my education from kindergarten to Master's degree level in Fine Arts, all my teachers, professors and mentors always told me that black and white are neutral colors, used to attain different hues of all kinds of color tones. When I look into the mirror, I see several hues of 'Nigger' chestnut colors from my head to my toes. Why? I was born and raised at longitude 5 degrees from the equator. Also, when I look at my better half, I see multiple hues of peach tones. She was born and raised at longitude farther north than mine and thus not exposed to almost half of a day's extreme heat radiating from the sun as early as 10:00 AM to almost 6:00 PM on some part of the Earth getting as hot as 120 degrees Fahrenheit temperature at times.

Furthermore, when I look at my two "Musketeers" who happen to be a girl and a boy, exciting *joie de vivre* engulfs me with praises to God Almighty. Thus gave birth to unflinching determination in me for raisons d'être my aspiration, which becomes an understatement for wanting to live forever. Too bad, we are making life span depreciate with unprovoked hate. Ergo, we are decreasing life expectancies, compared to when Adam lived up to 930 years. Breathless exclamation of surprise, when today's people live to be 90 years old, and that element of astonishment ejaculations which fill the air at funeral homes or eulogies, often expressed for much lower ages at times, of people exiting this world towards heaven's gate.

As a Christian, even with scientific breakthrough of cloning humans, I believe that God has something to do with our creation in putting us together, from the time our fathers and mothers met behind closed doors and begged God to bless them with children, which my Pastor refers to as "blessings of the womb." So I say that Barack Obama is what God has put together to effect noblesse oblige. For any one, who tries to put asunder what he lays his hands on to help people, becomes a doormat he walks all over. With those three world problems which President Obama seems to portray as significant positive attributes, he seems like someone who can mandate exemplification of God's will of peaceful melody through harmony, derived from respect and expression of genuine love between mankind from each other to each other of every world Immigrant can be achieved.

I submit that Obama is naturally and spiritually ascribed KKK, the three-letter word that depicts American ugly culture, which he could and already utilizing to invoke total forgiveness of old wounds from time immemorial. Otherwise, I don't think he would appoint his foe during the primaries for nomination to be the Democratic candidate for Presidency in 2008 as his Secretary of State, who according to the constitutional government rankings, could also become the President of the US, should President Obama becomes incapacitated.

Hope for world peace is in people finding unconditional love in each other. To find love in your fellow human being mandates total respect for whatever difference makes the opposite attract. If only to forgive totally, any upset that may have transpired, unfolding or intended consciously or otherwise contingent in human gestures of words, thoughts and deeds toward each other in the future, but only to have the meek and mild mind to offer humble friendship as reward for being just another human being, we would give births to genuine happiness and dance to profound music of lasting peace on earth. I pray that humanity will emulate the harmony of both the white and black keynotes of a piano dance to or church organ, to create beautiful melodies for generations in embryo of millennia years to come ad infinitum.

O! Stevie Wonder!! How does it go please? Sing it loud and clear.

"EBONY AND IVORY, LEAVING TOGETHER IN PERFECT HARMONY"

(1) D. James Kennedy, Ph.D.—State as forward in TOTAL FORGINESS by R.T. Kendall

DEDICATION

Solemnly to those who pray, wish and especially believe world peace is possible via "AUDACITY OF HOPE" and motivated by "CHANGE! YES WE CAN".

Emotionally to those who sacrificed their lives, parts of their being, blood, sweats, tears, time and efforts which guarantee America and her Immigrants abundant freedom.

INSPIRATIONAL ACKNOWLEDGMENT

Profound gratitude to Eunice and Michael III my two Musketeers, whose AfricAsiAmerican ethnicity, induced this book.

I refer to them as AfricAsiAmricans because their mother is a Taiwanese previously an Immigrant in Asia and I am originally a Nigerian Immigrant in West Africa but now, both of us are American Immigrants. Our two 'Musketeers' were both born in Rochester, New York State of the United States of America. Hence, I refer to both of them as AfricAsiAmericans as they are Immigrants on American soil, just like us and everybody else. Talk about second generation of American Immigrants.

This project also induced because I was late picking Eunice up from school when she was in grade numerological one. She was in tears, which made me lied that I stopped by the gas station to get some gas for our Ford mini van automobile. Never lie to your children. They'll make you feel less little than they are when they confront you with innocent inquisitiveness such as "Daddy, how fast does gas evaporate?" when she observed that my gas tank was less than a quart full after she got in but questioned me two weeks later.

I approached her with open arms pleading for the cause of her tears. She told me that her best friend's mother warned her not to play together with her daughter again. I made sure that she was not scared about the warning but asked her why she thought her friend's mother gave her such warning? She said the mother told her friend that she has 2-color skin. Whew! I exclaimed sigh of relief knowing that my lateness in picking her up was not the cause of her teary eyes. Otherwise, my Asian Damsel would chop stick my head when we got home. Eunice does not cry, trust me. As a girl, she was made one of Rahway Elementary School's Bully Buster in Grade 5. She is my first born beneficiary and I was over 50 when she made the triumphant birth ejaculation after more than 48 hours of induced expectation labor. She and I, beside the fact that I refused to get out of the house for about three weeks after was born that makes us act like wherever the snail goes does the crown shell, we still arm wrestle quite often.

Nonetheless, I was able to turn things around by asking her what I educated my children to be open minded about racial profiling and all the ugly scenarios that come with it and how to handle such heart broken exemplification from another world Immigrant, when thrown at them by those who can't comprehend their relationship to Adam and Eve. Then she remembered that I prepared her that it could be self made problem to some people if they feel jealous that other people are blessed with mixed skin colors. I told her that is exactly why some Immigrants can't wait to show off their bathing suits during Summer times, thousands of miles away from a pond, river, lake, sea, ocean or even Local Park or public swimming pool.

It thus reinforced my undying urge to keep helping uneducated minds as to how we are all blessed with endless hues of skin colors which to me reinforces amongst other factors, how really related we all are. On the sixth day of God's creation of the world, "And the Lord God formed man of the dust of the ground, and breathed into his nostrils the breath of life; and man became a living soul." Genesis 2:7. K J V. We made Him wish He did not create man in His own image, enough for Him to promise destruction of mankind, beast, creeping thing, and the fowls of the air in Gen. 6:6-7 as some of the heartless gestures of detrimental expressions to each other are fatal to peaceful cohabitation. Look into the mirror and slap yourself in the face if you are guilty. Go on henceforth and love your fellow earthly Immigrant because God loves you and so do I.

Finally, my innermost profound and genuine gratitude extended to Dean Olatunde Makanju Ph.D. and Dr. Adelaja Odutola Odukoya Ph.D. both from Lagos University in Nigeria, for comprehensive insights, in proof reading this project for publication. Let me just say big THANK YOU and hope you'd know how deep it came from the deepest of my pink throbbing muscle.

FOREWORD

I am Pentecostal in my spiritual belief, but far from being gifted enough to speak in tongues, or envision the future but adhere to history, the present and hope for a peaceful future. In essence, it means that my preconception of Mr. Obama is entirely spiritual in line with my religious belief and conviction to how I perceive the President. Please don't bang the heads on the wall to that. He is just like you and I, but how many you-s and I-s will make it to the Oval office as the Commander-In-Chief, especially the tough avenues and conditions which fate navigated him through. Father in absentia growing up, groomed by grand parents, grew up in a ghetto so to speak, but excelled at one of the greatest law schools on earth and ended up as the numerical Uno man in America.

I prayed that you have stumbled on and would read this book with open mind and curiosity to investigate possible directions in contributing to PEACE around the world of which President Barack Obama has set the train in motion with "AUDACITY OF HOPE". Otherwise, I humbly implore you to stop right here, close this book and throw it into your fireplace or get rid of it in any way your conscience may direct you. That is if you do not believe ALL human beings are created spiritually and thus can determine and manifest right from wrong in their thoughts, words and deeds to stop the chaos we delve into everyday. When God created us, He gave us the free will to determine our destinies, based on the tenet that God created you in His own Image to love and be peaceful with your fellow human beings and if you choose otherwise, I submit it contributes to causes of our world without peace and thus, your birth could be a waste at death.

"President and Mrs. Obama bring to the world exactly what it needs at this time in history and the evolution of humankind: Love, Support and caring. Perhaps, all of us should follow this magnificent example. We should strive to bring about an atmosphere of Peace and Harmony in all of our lives. Note: Its time to wake up people!!!."(2)

(2) reoraymond@yahoo.com
Comments on OBAMA RALLYM VCU Richmond 05/05/12

PREFACE

In one hand, "The human mind is a terrible thing to waste" and "God's time is the best" also induced my urge to pen this book. I thank God Almighty for the life He gave me and will not stop praying till God answers my supplications to Him for world peace.

I pay homage to people who come across the tenets I hold pure in this book. Ergo, this book is for those who are able to give room for other's source of inspiration, motivation, observations, ideas, discoveries, suggestions and the unflinching urge to affect some thoughts, thus believing that "two heads are better than one". Arguments to agree or otherwise contingent in positive or negative criticisms, I submit is your prerogative. I choose to enjoy expressing my freedom of speech literally.

My humble plead able offer is that this book is not the kind of book some people will tag along on long flights, rather than watch reruns of in-flight movies. Ergo, this work is especially for those who are motivated by "ODACITY OF HOPE". It is particularly for those who are encouraged by "CHANGE! YES WE CAN" to start making things better for all Immigrants on God's beautiful pleasance promenade earth and in so doing attain world's tranquility for mankind's peaceful existence.

Popularly for those who can confidently absorb that an achieved status of Nobel Peace Prize, awarded by world respected body of right thinking faculty is a token of appreciation and especially an acknowledgement of peace cadence. Peaceful deeds which recipients of such prestigious awards conferred upon, have established for the betterment of mankind. Positive deeds also believed will be established during his tenure as in the case of President Barack Hussein Obama peace maker in embryo caliber, which he has already hatched and set in motion, to be manifested again and again in thoughts, words and deeds throughout his historical presidency.

Also for those who can envision it a noteworthy gesture as a positive embodiment omen of world peace, when Queen Elizabeth II of Great Britain, who has never or would probably not make it a common and public practice to heartily hug an American First Lady like she embraced Michelle Obama. Americans can now continue to elect into the Oval Office, potential peacemakers. Presidents that would extend genuine amicable hands, to forge peace through respect, admiration and yes we are all descendants of Adam and Eve in this world. A President who could also make the world less frightening, by exposing and dealing diplomatically with people who nuclear arm race ambition to destroy the world is their goal, or people who are adamant in refusing to consider the possibility of world peace within human relationship.

Far from being an acknowledgement, this book is to anyone searching avenues for world peace illusion to evaporate and give mankind a chance at Garden of Eden experience. Meaning, if you can see my vision that Barack Obama is a likely avenue through which mankind can start thinking of how to make the world a little more peaceful and safer than what it is today, maybe we can enjoy what God intended for us, like when He created Adam and Eve and placed them in exotic promenade Garden of Eden, where they could have lived in peace with all the animals and wouldn't have to toil endlessly for a living or go through God's "Be fruitful and multiply" without agonizing pains related to child birth.

To those who can fantasize creation of beautiful harmonious melodies between human races, irrespective of difference in the endless color pigments of our skin.

To everyone that can conjure that better global economy is tied to World Peace in place.

To the world's good Samaritans who believe world peace will feed the hungry around the world. For example, if I am a caring Millionaire in any part of the world and know that I can travel to Ethiopia or any other place in the world to feed the poor children without being attacked by terrorists or any other groups that hate me being an American or a Christian or just being me, then World peace would be a beautiful thing to enjoy.

To those who can forgive, but difficult to forget trespassers in their lives. I say place them on Jesus feet on the cross and let His precious blood heal your wounds.

To those who are open minded to explore and manifest possibilities to create world peace. To you is my humbly imploration to share and exercise peacefully, gestures to mankind in any positive way you are so gifted.

Ironically to those turning blind eyes and close minds to the fact that incest is an ageless human culture, which prior ancient civilization during which time the mighty rescuer Moses, brought down the two tablets of the Ten Commandments from the mountains, after which it was suddenly classified immoral act. I just think that birth defects from such union justify reason to make it immoral. Now look at your spouse or playmate tonight and think deep, way back to Adam and Eve in the Garden of Eden, who were the only human beings God created physically in His own image. Maybe that thought can make you begin to become peaceful towards your fellow human beings. If Moses didn't bring the 2 tablets of the Ten Commandments and human beings are living like the 33 male and 23 female children of Adam and Eve who married each other to "Be fruitful and multiply" the world, wanting to make the world a more peaceful place would be the least world problem since we would be in cloud nine of world peace.

More ironically so, to those who consciously or otherwise contingent in their behavioral and other characteristic traits, exemplifying negative ethnocentric, idiosyncratic and illiteracy prone acts, with transparent betrayal of their imperfection human being qualities, lacking knowledge of evidence about the endless shades of pigments as abundant in human race are all God's blessings. I prayerfully direct your attention to a very ripe PEACH fruit and all the countless colors that grace its beauty. Look at it periphericallly as our spherical world, you'll find the color of your skin somewhere on it.

If world peace abounds, light peach color skinned people would be able to explore freely the urge to discover deep purple color skinned people around the world. Also, if you tour the Mediterranean coasts of Africa, some lighter skinned Britons would be amazed as to how tan skinned they are, compared to the lighter skinned inhabitants of those regions in North Africa. God blessed humanity with the richness of the sun which sedentary characteristic affects the earth's rotation on its own axis and 360 degrees rotations around the sun, established and mandated countless hues of mankind's color tones. Seeing will educate you and make you a believer. Plan your next vacation properly, you'll be convinced that the world needs to be friendlier and make World Peace, a priority of all earthly inhabitants.

On the other hand, maybe not for those who display religious hypocrisy, refusing to accept the tenets of the creation in Garden of Eden and why God did not stop on the 5$^{th.}$ Day but created man on the 6$^{th.}$ Day to reflect His own image and to enjoy the earthy paradise God intended for humanity we turned chaotic. Precisely, the book is not for Deists, those who do not believe God is in control of what He created and thus antagonize the possibility of world peace in any way they can.

Maybe not for those whose power hungry characteristics make them prone to religious antagonistic brainwashing, believing in suicidal and atrocious, dehumanizing missions? I pray for forgiveness and redemption of souls.

I hold steadfast the power of freedom of oratorical, literal and artistic rights of expressions with which we are blessed. In other words, take this book as I see it in my thoughts, observations and suggestions herein, or exercise your freedom rights the best you can. Just remember that I offer no apologies for trying to express how I feel that the 44th. President of the United States of America in my view is doing what will make American Democracy a utopian political and social example become realistic in the world, worthy of emulation by other Countries. You can always find me even at death, because I will always reinforce "Be ashamed to die until you have won some victory for humanity." (3). In other words, this book is my note book, evidence that I try to show my imagination of a possible peaceful world if we love each other unconditionally as immediate descendants of Adam and Eve did marrying each other, instead of jealously hating each other to extinction.

I submit that millions of Americans and people around the world, believe President Barack and Mrs. Michelle Obama are a couple of hope, couple of happiness, couple of safety, couple of motivation, couple of Inspiration and especially couple of "Change! Yes we can", who stopped unprovoked wars, brought home and established better protection, care of basic human needs and especially respect and honor for our brave men and women in uniforms guaranteeing our freedom. That's what a caring Commander-In-Chief and First Lady of a nation should prioritize in their Noblesse Oblige Oath to serve their Country.

Precious blood and lives should not always be the price for freedom, if no one tries to force you to sell or rob you of it.

Finally, this is also to appease my creative prowess, off limit to any pro or con judgment or criticism. Why? Because it is Godly ascribed quality with which any individual and every person is blessed during intussusceptions of my father's sperm, yoking with my mother's egg and fermented throughout embryogeny epoch, before "It's a boy!" triumphant natural ejaculation into the world by the Mid-Wife in attendance.

I hereby boldly state that one man's meat is another man's poison, in that individual expression via any medium such as writing, fabricating artworks, playing drums, etceteras, will be astonishing to some but dreadful and unappealing to others. Like me, I know as a human being, we always capitalize on our rights, with which every Immigrant around the world is privileged. Thanks to FREEDOM OF SPEECH, which I believe is extended to any type of creative expression, until someone tries to rob you of it or someone abuses his or hers, stepping on yours or vice versa you stepping on theirs. We love lawsuits don't we?

(3) Horace Mann—Founding President, Antioch College

CHAPTER 1

An Iceberg Spec of North America Immigrant Avalanche

That's my "home boy", Barack Obama. He is not even a full fleshed Immigrant by status like the filthy rich with silver spoon births in their mouths, people whose survival of the fittest Capitalism financial loot of the milk and honey seems restless in their pockets. Where are the termites when we need them to bore holes like the Wood Peckers on trees? Pay your fair share of income tax folks. Be it legal, illegal, smuggled or under the table income. Fair share is morally correct by American standard and at least makes me and fellow Immigrants think that whatever is good for the goose is good for the geese.

Barack Hussein Obama is just like one of us, extended Immigrants. Yes! Me, you reading this book if you claim Americanism like next door neighbor, your coworkers, church members, club Buddies and everybody else who claims US citizenship. Either by natural birth or caesarean section, asylum, voluntary or involuntary Alienation, naturalist instinct, through slavery or slave masters if still alive, or everybody else who is a descendant of the Earth's original two ancestors Adam and Eve in the Garden of Eden, which once upon a time, could be located somewhere in Iraq on African Continent. Oh yes, we are all Immigrants of "O Beautiful . . ." that is every human being on the face of the Earth on American soil is an Immigrant or a descendant or extended offspring of ancestral Immigrants. Except if you never left Iraq, directly or through contingencies of your parents, grand parents or their great, great grand parents, your ancestors. Any doubts? Clean up the attic and rummage through your family tree and write a short story for a Grade 7 Language

Arts project about how proud you are of your Immigrant status in North America. You might just be one of those who will not need a Kleenex or two, before you finish writing the story of how you got to the land of the free, to try your hands on the California Gold Rush, the origin of "The land of opportunity", my baseless wildest guess.

President Barack Obama, like the majority of us Americans is kind of different though. He is neither a descendant of a slave, nor is he in any way ever tasted any form of immigration stereotyping. By now, we all know that Papa Obama was a foreign Student from Kenya. Talk about sowing "Royal Oath" like in Eddy Murphy's "Coming to America" hilarious movie. Who could ever envision that Papa Obama's Royal Oath would grow "Against All Odds" to become The Commander-In-Chief of The United States of America? No wonder the Casino Magnate, just does not want to acknowledge Obama as a true son of the land, unlike him, a descendant of an Immigrant. Poor guy. Pardon me Mr. Trump, not poor as in Blackjack loots, but being humble and getting the facts straight. Obama's birth certificate is authentic from the viewpoints of his grand parents, father and especially his mother. If I am Barack Obama's mother a true American Immigrant, I would bark the authenticity of my son's American Immigrant legitimacy through his ear drums so hard; migraine headaches would wake him up for life.

How can I forget those born to foreigners by American citizens on American soil too? An iceberg of Immigrant avalanche—I submit that you now know someone like that. I hope you know that the great explorer Christopher Columbus, who discovered America, met the Red American Indians here, who also happened to have migrated from somewhere else like way North in Canada. Fascinating history, don't you think? Maybe I am guessing?

<u>Remembering who can claim American citizenry.</u>

The five unique groups of people comprising North American populate.

1. The Red Indians.
2. The Explorers.
3. The Slaves.
4. The Legal and Illegal Aliens.
5. The Extended Offspring of #s. 1- 4 above.

Unless you are on one of those temporary visitors' visas to the United States of America, there is an atom of Immigrant status in all Americans, regardless of how and where you were born on American soil. Should doubts invoke curiosity that kills the cat in you,—"The mind is a terrible thing to waste"—and I say that knowledge is the ingredient of wisdom. Put your parents, your grand or great grand parents to Ripley's "Believe It Or Not" episode, you'll never be the same again when it comes to patriotic arrogance, especially when you angrily tells somebody who is an American like yourself, to go back to where he or she came from. Ripley's believe it or not was a TV Show where mind bungling life events, stories and scenarios were brought to light in astonishing ways to educate the minds.

Hopefully, if you come out a new person, you'll see that all negative acts like racism, ethnocentrism, especially arrogance, etcetera, are products of idiosyncratic attributes of which you may be guilty. If so, you should be ashamed of hurting and causing another Immigrant like yourself such excruciating pains and deepest sorrows, with or by any of such atrocious acts which you ought to extricate yourself and make America a better place for all her Immigrants en masse. The food for thought here is we are all Adam and Eve offspring to the countless power, as in math when you find a quotient to the $3^{rd.}$ $4^{th.,}$ or more powers.

The world is too big for some people to comprehend what it's all about originally. God spent six days creating paradise of beautiful exquisite natural grandeur called Earth. I figured out in my imaginative fancy, that He sat back after a hard day's work on the $5^{th.}$ Day and saw that all the wonders He has created are beautiful and was very pleased indeed.

On day six, He started to think that he would put a 'Gardener—Adam' in His own image to take care of His creations, while he waters it with "Gentle rain from Heaven"—like in 'Merchant of Venice'—so that healthy growth would flourish. Also, He blessed the Earth with some sunshine to give all the living things in it their beautiful skin pigments from darkest purple to lightest peach hues. We all ought to carry our numerous complexions with pride and especially gratefulness, rather than whine and hate each other creating alienation between mankind because of our different but unique skin colors. I suggest you copy the late King of Pop—Michael Jackson's pigment purification strategy. Lock yourself up in ultra violet sonic coffin from September until April of every year, if you live in the part of the world which is blessed with blistering Santa Clause Ho Ho Ho Season. Come out between May and August, to partake in the abundant blessings of Photosynthesis which produces chlorophyll for radiant color tones with which humanity is blessed.

After God created Adam from mud and breathed the breath of life into the nostrils of the sculpture He created in His own image, it then became a living soul like you and I as stated in the Bible book of Genesis 2: v.7. He saw that Adam was lonely. Out of Adam's ribs He took one out and created a companion named Eve, to comfort Adam in the Garden of Eden. God then blessed them, and God said unto them, "Be fruitful, and multiply the Earth". Genesis 1: v. 28. Believe it or not, we are all very long extended offspring of those two original people God created physically. Does that mean we are all related one way or the other? You might be surprised at what you find via your ancestral tree. I wish you happy hunting cum good luck from my heart, you compatriot Immigrant one.

By the way, I think God did not intend incest to be ungodly or immoral, until Brother Moses brought down the 2 Tablets of the Ten Commandments God wrote by fire, which then counter act Gods will for us. Monkey Kingdom scenarios, where you can just go about your enjoyment of the Garden of Eden style of living and be fruitful and multiply with your sister, brother and other relatives, then became immoral and a crime today. I think that God figured He probably should scatter us by throwing us into state of confusion with different languages. At the scene in Babylon where we were trying to create a tall tower to go ask God why we have so much problems in the world He created for us to enjoy. He threw at us different languages and thus distant us from calling each other brothers and sisters or Auntie and Uncle, so as to declare incest immoral.

History will always repeat itself when it comes to how the United States of America began. I think this is true when there is a law that allows so many thousands of people on Immigration scholarships to become American Patriots and taste cow milk with bee honey every year. This means that the Constitution realized the importance of Immigration as the basis for America's multi blessings in terms of every aspect of its existence that makes it the melting and greatest pot of the world. I think that is one of the reasons why America can continue to be the greatest Country in the world as I termed it the world's Capital or oasis, serving as a pleasant relief and refuge of the world. Wow!

The Constitution implicitly educates us on how to make the world love and respect America only if we wholeheartedly execute the Constitution's verbalism.

I concluded then that there are five types of people that comprise our populace. The America Indians are the first settlers, who themselves migrated from the North somewhere like Canada. Then the great Voyager Christopher Columbus on something like the Mayflower Boat who discovered America, then rounded up the Indians and patched them and put them up in Indian Reservations across America. The third groups of people are the African slaves who were tricked into buying and exchanging goods but later captured and packed like sardines on typical "Mayflower," the kind of ship in which Pilgrim Fathers sailed from England to America in 1620. Except that some of those kinds of ships were used in smuggling forcefully, the African slaves into America some of who ended up growing lots of cotton in the south. Some were later hung by their necks with ropes or upside down by their feet, dangling from tree branches. I think those who did that were from the line of or inherited Abel's senior brother Cain's attribute, because I read in the Bible that Cain killed his brother Abel for jealousy which also constitute hate, the human terminal disease of imperfection.

Barack Obama looks like what God has put together; no right thing faculty should try to put asunder. See how he bulldozes his ideas through dark alleys of vehement oppositions. Nevertheless, I realized that he is not immortal and like all mortals, that is all of us on planet earth as her Immigrants, will pay the curse Adam brought on to us all when he tasted the forbidden fruit from the center of the Garden of Eden, hopefully after he gets to be a great grand father. Do I hear Amen? Amen anyone? Yes you, Oh yes, you too. We thank you Allah, thank you Yahweh, and thank you Jehovah. We give God glory and praise the Lord of heavenly hosts. Amen. No apologies for where my spirit directs me.

Regardless, I profess that by the time President Obama leaves the Oval Office as the Commander-In-Chief, American history books and records may not adequately do justice to how he opened our eyes appropriateness. Brightened our eyes to focus on possibilities which humanity ought to make prima facie priority, in finding ways to try and solve the three major human errors we keep letting them make life's *joie de vivre* a fantasy for us. No matter how healthy, wealthy and educated, we are in denial if we do nothing towards world peace, world peace will not make itself possible. President Barack Obama is well on his way to making us realize that world peace could be a possible reality. Note worthy facts to mention a few of his peace keeping achievements include stopping unprovoked Iraq war which he was against from the time he was a Senator. He did away with the world's most notorious Terrorist. As a President who must protect all citizens regardless of their interests as long as there is no law against them, he accepted the Gay community as they are. People may not like it; at least the President's tolerance of their way of life made it difficult if not unlawful harassing them anymore.

"Believe it or not" Ripley's TV Episodic Series says World peace is within mankind reach if we say something when we see anything, any person, or any strange event that tickles our fancy. When you observe an abnormality, call for help for someone or yourself before people pay undue price for creating alienation, rather than friendly gesture of "Hello and howdy today", while passing your fellow human being on the streets. If no response, the more reason to be concerned and alarm raised for your fellow human being. You will reap the fruit of your labor, positive or negative speaking.

Positively speaking, no one can live in this world alone. From the moment your "Sweet Mother, A no go forget you for this suffer wey you suffer for me ye e", (4) ejected you like a torpedo bundle of joy from her, till the time you are reading this book, you probably did not prepare or harvest the food you cooked for breakfast this morning, lunch or supper yesterday or will prepare by yourself tomorrow and in the future. Did you manufacture the automobile you spend precious hours washing and showing off in it as if you can even change the oil? How about when you graduated from college if you had the opportunity to go through one, did you start working in your own company right away or you got paid weekly, bi-weekly or monthly working your sweat up the ladder while laboring or toiling in someone else's establishment? I even declare that you probably couldn't revive yourself when you were having a seizure, heart attack, choking or mere headache that often send you rummaging your mumbo jumbo overcrowded medicine cabinet, for remedies like Bayer's Aspirin or Advil. I like to say you are too far from being a Pharmacist. You can't be a Pilot and a Locomotive train engine driver at the same time, or possibly the Priest who pronounced you 'Husband and Wife' before your supposedly public first smooch. I know you can think of countless other things we do in our daily life existence, I just hope they make you believe that nobody can live in this world alone. Ergo, why are you not putting in your fair share to make it peaceful for yourself and everyone else?

After all, we are all Immigrants in this world in any part of it you call your Country. People like us once upon a time, celebrated over 900 birthdays. Due to today's atmospheric pollution which I believe angers God, if someone lives beyond 90 or even 70 year's life span, there comes opportunity to show off spending arrogance. I know some cultures in which celebrations for such longevity often cause the family turmoil for extravagant spending over the dead body they did not take good care of when alive. God often caution us with the wroth of earthquakes, tornadoes, hurricanes, mud sledges etceteras, to remind us of Noah's Arc, even though He promised not to destroy the earth with water again, yet we turn deaf ears and minds to aim at world peace. Repent folks. You will be granted eternal joy with your last breath.

(4) Nigerian Musician—Prince N. Mbarga

CHAPTER 2

2008 Democratic Primaries to November Presidential Election

Pentecostal Change of heart to "Audacity of Hope" anticipation

This book is also induced by some ascribed and achieved natural and spiritual attributes, of the kind of unique person I am spiritually convinced to believe President Barack Hussein Obama is blessed atypical. Prior his Presidency, we had 43 Presidents, from the first "Uncle Sam" Papa George Washington, through Abraham Lincoln the January 1, 1863 Emancipator to the 43rd. President who lavished $480 Billions chasing ghostly WEAPONS OF MASS DESTRUCTION in Iraq, none of them could conjure the three main world problems which are making world peace illusive to us all as much as President Barack Obama's atypical attributes invoke. In American Presidential history, no other American President was a Muslim and Christian affiliation ascribed him that could appeal to all religions, neither was any American President a bi-Racial to promote peace amongst human races as Obama, nor was there any American President who could use detrimental KKK culture as a positive possibility to induce the spirit of forgiveness to those who committed such atrocities to humanity, even in their graves.

When I ask people to name what they think the #1 MAJOR WORLD PROBLEM is, I always hear something like bad economy, starvation, several wars, bad politics and politicians or some bad Heads of States and Presidents or Dictators of other countries around the world, which I label secondary problems to the problem I construe as #1 major world problem in next paragraph. Furthermore, inquiry about what people see as #2 MAJOR WORLD PROBLEM usually also draws typical answers, to which I always associate minor world problems the world can take care of, solve, improve or even eradicate, if what I submit to be our major problems in this world could be fixed.

My #1 MAJOR WORLD PROBLEM is religious conflicts around the world, especially between Christianity and Islam. Anybody ever wonders why Middle East peaceful harmonious habitation by its Arabian inhabitants is so unbelievable impossible, after so many years, make that centuries of reckless, unwarranted, unwanted and avoidable senseless bloodsheds because of religious conflicts between Islam and Christianity/Judaism? My # 2 MAJOR WORLD PROBLEM is racial disharmony around the world. To this, I attach a #3 MAJOR WORLD PROBLEM, which gave birth to slavery, prejudice, ethnocentrism, idiosyncrasy, power hunger, heartlessness, disrespect and many other sinful acts against fellow human beings. These three awful man made negative institutions or cultures, feed us with hateful alienation from each other and make the thought of being descendants of Adam and Eve a taboo in so many living hearts and souls. All these derail us from thinking on how to make the world a better place. Not just for us, but for our children and many generations in embryo of many millennia years to come.

Do I think the world can be peaceful if we have someone to educate us or show that peace between Muslims and Christians or Jews and the PLO in the Middle East or between other religions is achievable? I'll put my life savings on it that I do. I also submit that if we can emulate the harmony between the white and black keynotes of piano or church organs to create beautiful melodies, maybe we will learn to mingle more peacefully. Let humanity stops being adamantly strong headed for a minute, to simple nature's facts, which plants enjoy with their various tints or hues of greens and other exotic colors through photosynthesis. The inexhaustible production of abundant chlorophyll for their beauties can also make us enjoy and appreciate our countless hues or tones of skin colors, which the sunshine blesses us with.

My Pentecostal up bringing makes me submit that President Barack Obama may not be anything close to Jesus Christ, because he used to smoke cigarettes and I think if not that he was the President, he would sue the guy who elbowed his lips or eye brow playing basketball. Jesus Christ came peacefully and shed his precious blood to try and appease His Father the Creator of Heaven and Earth, to forgive our careless destruction of the world He created for us to enjoy as He commanded us to "Be fruitful and multiply". Nonetheless I submit that President Obama might just have the golden key to unlock the door for humanity to start dialectic dialogue negotiating world peace.

I know some people who were born by a Muslim father and a Christian mother or many other cross ethnicity or inter-religions ejaculated children like me and my two Musketeer AfricAsiAmericans, but I think we should seize this opportunity of Barack Obama's atypical American Presidency, to believe we could broker world peace as he is ironically doing. Check this out. Barack Obama is a Christian who grew up under the influence of Islam. Could that be the reason why both religions and many others, welcomed him with open arms when he took a world tour before he became the President of the United States of America? How about how would you describe the omen which ascribed him a beautiful melody of the sensual harmonies between a dark skin father from ***K***enya and a light skin mother from America with affiliation to ***K***ansas? And fate named him Barac***k.*** Notice the three big ***K***s? Watch how they play to his mission in life as someone with peaceful weapons to try and make the world harmonious next.

They bring me to the good old America's "Star Spangle Banner" "O, Say can you see . . ." and when you connect it to "America the Beautiful" "Oh Beautiful . . ." makes goose bumps sprout vehemently from my pores. Those two songs make me feel very proud being a naturalized American soil Immigrant. Regrettably though, my patriotic ecstasy becomes muddy with rueful shame when confronted with racial blemish of *KKK* in American culture Human beings hiding under white hoods, lynching fellow human beings because of different tones or hues of the same human skin pigments. It makes me feel or look like a square peg in a round hole, having no adequate words to express how very shameful and rueful all real patriotic American Immigrants ought to feel, when in reminiscent mode of that era as a very dark epoch of American ugly culture, camouflaged by snow white robes and cone hoods. Again, Barack Obama is naturally ascribed a racial mandate of peacekeeper prowess, with no choice but to appeal to all humanity. White, black, yellow, green or purple as if any one has ever seen any human being with any of those colors. Minus white and Black shades, which are neutral? I think anyone will go to the bathroom in daylight when a really white or black creature approaches or meets you alone in a dark alley or even in day light. Let's be real and avoid some nonsensical and detrimental figure of speech name calling. It makes *tout le monde* of world Immigrants look and act ***S***atan's ***T***reading ***U***pon ***P***eople's ***I***ntellectual ***D***isorder against each other. Mercy O Lord.

Due to my political illiteracy and don't give a hoot to elections even though I always capitalize on my voting rites, but for not knowing Barack Obama prior to the political wars of 2008 Primaries between him and Mrs. Hillary Rodman Clinton, I started out rooting for Mrs. Clinton. My rooting for her was influenced by the positive legacy of President William Jefferson Clinton—the ardent antique Saxophonist, her husband's exceptional balancing of the budget and leaving surplus for American people act of his two term-Presidencies, was especially exoteric. Unlike esoteric presidencies of some President's tenures, which dried up the surplus President Clinton, left behind. Little did we realize that such drying up the surplus placed America, Americans and the world as a whole on a path of destruction which could have been a catastrophic history of greatest recession the world ever experienced to cause deepest depression all mankind would rather not experience. Whew! Obama showed up as a bad economy ghost buster.

Over **B**earing **A**mbition **M**ust **A**bide by "Change! Yes We Can", came to the rescue with Bailouts here, bailouts there and more reversed bailouts as in making companies pay for negligence and crooked awarded government business contracts, are just a tip of an iceberg of better things to come under Barack Obama's Presidency. I believe somebody could hold BP responsible for the oil disaster in the Gulf much earlier by not approving unsafe drilling procedures, but typical culture must make way for atypical command of "Change! Yes We Can" authority of President Barack Obama's *modus operandi* to manifest "Audacity of Hope" for ALL Americans. That includes the Republicans, Independents and or all other party agents, who would rather not capitalize on their citizenship rights, but prefer to practice abstention of Zombie-like "follow follow" culture, as the late African Beat Pioneer Fela Anikulapo Kuti of Nigeria in West Africa puts it in rhythmical lyricism.

By the way, music originated from Africa; if you have not already figured it out that the Garden of Eden from where we all migrated was situated somewhere in Iraq located in Africa. Also, if you ever wonder how African Immigrant women can dance with such graceful forms and vibrate to rhythm dynamics the way they do, get that CD titled "Zombie" by Fela Anikulapo Kuti. You will naturally shed some unwanted flabbiness, dancing to the Afro Beat CD. Pardon me Madam Jane Fonda ET Monsieur Richard Simons and all other exercise and diet Gurus out there. I don't mean to tell you to move over; you guys are doing wonderfully great, and helping people lose those double pound digits for good healthy living. Enjoy your millions, it is the 24/7 maxim of American Capitalism.

So far in President Obama's first term, he has already proved beyond doubts that he is not a typical American President in history. He commands atypical in being the first dark skinned American President and still counting positive missions accomplished, to soften world tension at fear, with regards to ending unprovoked war in Iraq. It was an aggression that was obviously a transparent example of power abuse which cost Tax payers at least $10 Billions a month for 4 years, i.e. $480 Billions. I can not but express feelings of deepest sorrow, for the lives of about 5,000 of our brave men and women in uniforms, not to mention heart felt pain for those tens of thousands of innocent Iraqi civilian lives of men, women and children, particularly all over the world, with increased worldwide terrorism at the time. Thank God Almighty terrorism seems to be facing a Commander-In-Chief who gives no preference to the maxim that has no respect, regard, but unprovoked hatred for humanity.

I am still saddened by hypocritical gestures I encountered from some of my Christian friends when I withdrew from supporting Mrs. Clinton's candidacy during the primary nomination. Especially when she implied she would consider Barack Obama for running mate as Vice President. Nothing could be odder, I thought. Some of my Christian family friends I respect and adore very highly stopped answering my telephone calls, even if it's just the Merry Christmas Ho! Ho!! Ho!!! The popular Yuletide greetings or the likes couldn't prevent shutting me off because I voted for a person that they claimed supports abortion in his campaign. I voiced that I never heard him categorically stated he supports abortion. Neither did he say he would not but allocate Federal Government or Tax Payer's funds to foot abortion bills, nor did he ever give women thumbs up for indiscriminate extra marital misbehavior, which could force unnecessary agonizing decision making moments to kill or not to terminate the unborn.

All I was hearing rhetorically loud and clear by Barack Obama was the need to educate women and men to respect themselves, until they are ready, willing and capable of parenting diapers change dramas. Rather than face the dilemma of tough brain anguish on aborting innocent lives, "prevention is better than cure" has to be put in place to educate citizens. Especially if you are not ready, capable and willing to take parenting bull by the horn, either as single mama or worse still a free spirit Casanova as in American Gigolo's Richard Gere, one heck of An Officer and a Gentleman Star, or maybe as in the Werewolf in London movie. President Obama explicitly implied during the primaries that Citizens should look before leaping into the habit of indiscriminate exhibition of pervasive shame.

Regardless of what I thought then, ratio 2-1 in the millions decided America's fate as to the choice. Democracy enforced which candidate is humanitarianly better suited for the Oval Office of the White House on Pennsylvania Avenue. All I can now say is that the first 4 years was not easy mending our wounds from fear and insecurity, but we are experiencing a little peaceful atmosphere around the world and economy is a little slow in recovery. Nonetheless, London 2012 Olympics is peaceful tribute to all the Olympians, people around the world. None notable terrorist scenario or threats was Godly. Let us be thankful for the peace of mind during the Olympics and since Obama is holding that magic peace wand, I am sleeping a little more peaceful. I pray you feel safe too for the next 4 years at least.

CHAPTER 3

As an Atypical American President

On Home Front

Call it *political dogma;* Barack Hussein Obama is composed of three significant ingredients for recipe mankind needs to bake world peace cake of harmonious delicacy for humanity.

President Barack Hussein Obama in my book justifies if I may, unapologetic capitalism on being "first this, first that" atypical American President, in mandating CHANGE! YES WE CAN" and providing avenues to make "AUDACITY OF HOPE" a reality for ALL Americans, even if you are Warren Buffet or homeless pan handler we labeled Mr. Golden Voice, discovered on the street corner by a radio station. I don't know the counts, regarding the number of male employees who turned out to being the head of their female Bosses nucleus families, via Holy matrimonial unions. From several lunch date refusals through the Alter, came two bundles of adoring joys Marla and Sasha for the man with Ms. Michelle's feminine enticements on his masculine mind soonest she was commissioned to monitor his legal professional prowess. Talk about messing around on the job. Whew! Homeboy, some powerful audacity of bravery you maneuvered in rescuing Michelle from likely suitors. Who took the tab that memorable lunch date that made you follow Adams foot steps in biting the forbidden fruit? I could hear him now "Mind your business dude and leave my girl out of it too". No offense boss, my hands behind my back. I am just kidding. No "MIB" at my door. OK?

Need I continue to list Barack Obama's bold and brave atypical presidential model accomplishments so far?

American history books would not do adequate justice to his Presidential Curriculum Vitae.

Since the original or first Immigrants on American soil are the Red Indians who migrated from the North, I can then submit that Canada is older than America as a country? Correct me if I am wrong. He who is tired of learning is not fit to live. I really did not go into research for this book; I just scribbled what my three brains Medulla Oblongata, Cerebellum and Cerebrum fed me about my subject's presidential persona, through Daily News Papers, Internet stories and citizens' tweets and comments on various articles of importance.

Nonetheless, this book may be tagged incomplete without some of his history making deeds, which make Obama an atypical "Afro American", especially rising from the Harlem of Michigan in Illinois "Ghetto." RIDE ON MY BROTHER. Forgive me, BLACK PANTHERS epoch comes to mind.

As I was saying reader, President Obama's atypical first term, boasts of so many crucial American problems solved scenarios of deeds that can be labeled 'executive mandates'. Can you name anything, suggestions, ideas or even just taking the first girls Sasha and Malia out for ice cream, or burger bites at a local restaurant that was not talked against? People always want to question or vehemently but fruitlessly fight against his CHANGE! YES WE CAN" and AUDACITY OF HOPE, especially by opposition Republics, Independence and all others, especially some Christians who still hypocritically refuse to pray for their leaders as ordered by Jesus Christ? What some Christians will do against our Lord and Savior Jesus Christ couldn't be more surprising. Who could ever envision that Crystal Cathedral Ministry will be torpedoed into the abyss of Catholic Diocese Empire and in the tune of something like over $50 millions "In God We Trust" prints? I wonder if any of those went to humanitarian deeds for charitable contributions as I did when I became an Eagles' club member many years ago.

I don't know how Canadians managed to twist their government's hands and got all her Citizens insured medically. I just have to credit Barack Obama's intuitions for migrating that benefit to American soil after all these show off years of being the richest country the world has ever seen. I hope you realize that Obama approved some tax credits, so that every American can at least buy a working health Insurance, rather than force the government to keep shelling some In God We Trust Uncle Sam to gold digging health Insurance gluttons. The mechanism some groups employ to keep the deficit blamable on Obama, so as to keep more Americans begging and stay being Government welfare addicts. One point of interest on the health care vote is that the ALL MUST get Health Insurance Law of Obamacare passed miraculously by an unlikely Justice's vote, which was by all beliefs, supposed to oppose it. I hope those who read this book are not among those who still think whatever President Obama puts together, must be put asunder. Remember a doormat emits the most aroma of nasal hate and often cause indigestion.

Thank God, Obamacare makes it possible to avoid wasting your hard-earned money on Gas-x or Pepto-bismol drugs.

I know you will never forget who stopped $10 Billions a month for 4 years waste, trying to get Saddam Hussein on the pretence of finding non-existing WEAPONS OF MASS DESTRUCTION which everybody was aware, as confirmed by the most intelligent agency establishment respected—make that feared around the world. My Gosh, that's $480 Billions in a President's second term in the Oval Office, burnt, worst than burning American flags by haters. If you told me that Saddam Hussein was the weapon of mass destruction, it would be enough justification for me to enroll as NAVY SEAL with my gray hair. We could have dealt with the dictator without losing some 5,000 brave men and women in uniforms and many thousands more innocent Iraqis, sacrificed and wasted unjustly in unprovoked war in Iraq. Can you come up with a worst atrocity, which can be classified obvious exemplification of power drunkenness that could fit war crimes against humanity?

There seems to never have been any other American President who had Islamic upbringing and then converted to Christian belief. In my upbringing as a Christian, I have lived through years of witnessing Islamic religion celebrations, marred with Islamic children staging and waging animal fights against each other during the festival after Ramadan fasting periods. Muslim children bring to playgrounds, rams their parents saved a whole year salaries to be sacrificed for after Ramadan feasting festival and forced them to lock horns against each other at times to disastrous ends, shedding animal blood and breaking their horns all in the name of Allah I use to ask? Where is the peaceful connotation of Islam here I use to wonder.

Is this in line with how history relays the creation of Islam and why some Muslims believe they will become martyrs if they commit suicides, taking innocent peoples' lives as they untimely cause extinction of their God given lives? I find it very ironic when people of Islamic faith try to portray it as a religion of peace, even though, I am not at liberty as a Christian to judge what other people hold sacred. Nevertheless, I wonder if it means Islam is void of spiritual connection to God even though they worship Him as the Allah. The ironic innuendo as it relates to Barack Hussein Obama is that he was exposed to Islamic doctrine during his early years on earth, but grew up to proclaim Christianity as his religion. This atypical hermaphroditic presage of both Islam and Christianity achieved attributes, I believe puts him in a Peacemaker Driver position to appeal for religious truce and stop millions of wasted lives continuity. Lack of this kind of peace between these two religions, have claimed brutally for many centuries gone bye.

It is not a fable that there is no other religion in this world that can claim, take solace or boast of a Spiritual Savior as in Jesus Christ the Savior of mankind. The Bible gave accounts of a Savior Jesus Christ who died and shed precious blood on the cross as a Lamb of God His Father, for the redemption of humanity's grievous sins against the Creator Almighty God. I think some of the terrorists believe that if they sacrifice their lives committing suicide bombings, they will become Martyrs. Religiously as a Christian, I wish they repented with their last breaths for forgiveness to be welcomed next to God Almighty the Allah, where there is no weeping and gnashing of teeth, but alleluia chorus all the way. I know there are Islamic songs; I just wonder how Allah reacts to them in heaven. I can't wait to find out and that is in God's time I submit. Don't even think about it, I am ready to face God Almighty at any time he calls for me to pay my debt.

Christianity as I know it is faith by spirituality which lives in every creature on earth. Yes! You and every living thing, even plants could be spiritual. Spiritual attributes by faith, confirmed on how Jesus Christ came to this world, lived 33 years like the number of sons Adam had in his 930 years of life, performed many miraculous wonders no other human being will ever emulate, regardless of breath taking scientific evolutions. If you have an open-heart or any other surgery and survived, it's because you had a defective organ and scientific technology repaired it. When you die the real death, which was a curse mandated on us by God, no science or scientist can breathe the breath of life into you. God is still against our original sin committed by Adam and Eve for fallen to the temptation of the snake called the devil, thereby disobeyed God's commandment to stare clear of the forbidden fruit, Science or any other technological procedure can not compare with Jesus

Christ miracles. So, Immaculate Conception, the dogma that the Virgin Mary was conceived without the stain of original sin, makes Jesus Christ a Spirit in flesh, which He shares with us. I was careful by not saying technological miracle, which in its innovations warrants praise though.

I don't know of any other human being like Jesus Christ when He was in the likeness of us human beings, before dying and claiming His Spiritual greatness, to appeal to God Almighty as His Father, to forgive us that we know not what we did to Him on the cross. So was the moment when Judas Iscariot betrayed Him. Mark 3:19, a disciple who made himself a decoy to the slaughter of the Lamb, KKK epoch was borne by his act. I think those who made that act known many centuries later, must have followed suit sacrilegiously in the ways they parted the world, paying their debts to God's curse on humanity because of the original sin committed by Adam and Eve, tasting the forbidden fruit. I know my God and Savior Jesus Christ must have forgiven them all. After all, His precious blood is sufficient for all our sins.

The religious exposition in this chapter is because I perceive President Obama to be atypical indeed, someone who is indirectly using his dual religious affiliations as a Muslim by parental mandate and as a Christian by self proclamation and obviously positive deeds to the betterment of humanity to implore all Americans and the world, that religion is a right of passage through life, and we should give no preference to the maxim of hate. Rather, it should create avenue for peaceful exemplification amongst humanity as to the peace both religions claim to bring to the world.

More important atypical quality of Obama's Presidency on the home front issues shows that Barack Hussein Obama and Democratic Teams have accomplished and achieved deeds to benefit all Americans one way or the other, almost everyday of the week of every month of the year since he took office. I am tempted to reference a list, but felt it would propagate page volume of the book. Hence I implore your curiosity to rummage Barack Obama Achievements and Accomplishments.mht for several pages of his full fleshed list of accomplishments and achievements atypical to any other past Presidents in only first term tenure.

To entice you for more of Obama's accomplishments and achievements of his first term alone, here are some deeds I consider aim at improving life and geared towards peaceful cohabitation of American Immigrants and habitat Immigrants of other parts of the world en masse

Insurance policy amount and terms enhanced for severely disabled veterans—October 14, 2010.

Service members receiving relocation are protected from early termination fees for certain contacts and residential leases—October 14, 2010

Schools and communities provided resources to utilize local farms and gardens to provide fresh produce for school programs.—December 13, 2010. Thanks to the "green thumbed" First Lady of the White House inaugural gardening motivation I guess. Go Michelle, 2016 first female Commander-In-Chief is waiting for you. Is it hyperbolic or ironic dream? Remember, dreams come true.

$1.5 billion awarded to some 75, 000 black farmers who were victims of discrimination in applying for farm loans from 1983 to 1997.—December 8, 2010. Who was the President then?

$3.4 Billion settlement for Native Americans against the US government arising from incorrect accounting for royalties on mineral leases.—December 8, 2010.

Number of eligible children enrolled in school meal programs increased by approximately 115,000 students.—December 13, 2010

$136 billion in tax relief for 2 million middle class households through patch to the Alternative Medium Tax for 2010 & 2011.—December 17, 2010.

$111 billion in tax relief for workers by reducing social security payroll tax from 6.2% to 4.2 for 2011.—December 17, 2010.

$40 billion in tax credits for college students and lower income families with children.—December 17, 2010.

Gay and Lesbians, some may be Christians allowed to serve openly in the military.—December 22, 2010, but when Obama gave no indication of rejecting and objecting their type of romantic relationship, some Christian and other religion hypocrites grumbled.

Number of US and Russian nuclear warheads deployed reduced by two-thirds by 2017—February 5. 2011 and this foreign policy novice, goes about calling Russia America's #1 enemy.

The number of US and Russia strategic nuclear missile launchers, agreed to be reduced by half by 2017—February 5, 2011. Can some please tell this 2012 Presidential candidate contender, that America and the whole world is beginning to shiver thinking of dead old Cold War race may be rekindled when he is labeling Russia as America's #1 enemy? My Gosh Mitt! It shows how much you love all those people in your extended family picture, trying to make Putin wake up from the wrong side of his bed. Pleeeeeeeeez! Stay away from the white house. You are banned from thinking of the Oval Office.

For more kindness to humanity deeds of President Barack Obama, please click your PC @ Barack Obama Accomplishments & Achievements.mht. I pray you cast your vote wisely in November.

CHAPTER 4

Barack Hussein Obama as Commander-In-Chief

Foreign Front

I have witnessed people parachuted from flying planes before and thought I have seen it all for impressive bravery, especially when it's a woman. Until a whole Commander-In-Chief of the United States of America, was dropped off on a US war ship from a jet fighter. It reminded me of when Prince Williams stole his would-be Duchess of Cambridge's heart, by single handedly landing a loaded assault Royal Navy Helicopter on his soon to be In-Law's estate in England. Wow! Some silver mouthed and spooned damsel lucky Lady DI's Daughter-In-Law Prince Williams nested over there.

President Barack Obama in his first term alone already proved that being a Veteran is not a curriculum vitae requirement for American Presidency. It does not have to include veteran ability or non for that matter, to be a Commander-In-Chief from the Oval Offices, especially when it comes to snatching the most wanted Terrorist in the world without losing a single drop of blood from any of our brave men during the raid. Americans and the rest of the world should debate and weigh in on giving movie stars, wealthy people or anybody who sold their countries' job overseas, to vie for the Presidency of their countries again. I just think that anybody who exports or out source American jobs which fellow Americans depend on, should not be given opportunity to even visit the White house, how much more campaign to become her President. Noble Character exemplification, coupled with outstanding record of helping humanity achieve world peace, should be prima facie requirements amongst other qualifications in service to humanity for Presidency. Just like I think that you can't stand an arrogant person even if he pays your bill or puts food on your table and clothes you, so also do other nations' leftist, rightist or extremist would rather terrorize you first by throwing stinky shoe for unfounded arrogance.

As the Commander-In-Chief, Barack Hussein Obama is atypical in numerous positive ways to forge or broker world peace, based on his exquisite spiritual and ascribed attributes the world needs to think that peace is possible on earth.

Examples of his brave deeds include ending an unprovoked war in Iraq and bringing our brave men and women in uniforms back home. To me, that alone does not only signify subscription to peace on the long run, but telling the whole world that war in general barricades peaceful process. The fact that he also dealt away with Osama Bin Laden the world most wanted terrorist without losing a single American soul during the raid by the NAVY SEALS on Bin Ladin's compound in Pakistan, to avoid possible hurdle against possible peace, makes it worth considering as a token of get the bad guy out without inflating angry battle. Pakistan may say she was insulted, but I feel in my heart that peaceful Pakistani Immigrants of the world were quietly happy that an unscrupulous humankind hater thorn is plucked from their flesh. Rather than invade Iran that is nuclear power proud against International objection, Obama is working with Allies to reinforce sanctions that could cripple Iran's motive for nuclear program. Same scenario with North Korea which despite Washington's objection to its nuclear test lunches, Obama has played it down diplomatically that the world is hoping North Korea would not cross Obama's red line and fans the fire of world war that will definitely end any attempt towards world peace. Ironically also, Obama has indirectly but peacefully removed some Dictators abusing human rights in their countries like Mubarak of Egypt and Gadhafi of Libya by just telling them publicly from the Oval Office via the red phone with his feet on the most effective action table in the world, to step down and thereby started democratic considerations for their succeeding governments. Again, no American blood shed, but when sinners are punished innocent people partake was manifested in those countries, with reference to tens of thousands of innocent people perished during their transitions to Democracy.

Gone is January 1, Y2K when I expected the heavens to open and present us with the peaceful and forgiving Messiah. Nowadays, I am of the opinion that I may not see Jesus Christ come back in my lifetime to 'judge the quick and the dead', but I declare that Barack Obama has set the stage for world peace. The fact remains that Obama ironically mediates peacefully between Islam, Judaism, Christianity, Zionism and Buddhism, which are some of the major world religions that divide us to brutal extinction. Otherwise some human rights abuse that America vehemently condemns would not have allowed a blind Chinese dissident agreement negotiation for him to study in America to be completed on May 19, 2012 but for the birds to fly away with and further tightening tension of hate. Obama is also an example of beautiful melodies, which poor and bad taste figure of speech on White and Black human beings, should emulate to create harmony. These two atypical attributes cum the dreadful KKK sign of hate, like the dreadful 666 number of the beast he portrays with ease, are indicative demand for foreignness. No other American President in history could ever boast of Obama's ascribed and achieved fateful weapons of peace mandate for world's Immigrants, that includes all human beings alive. That makes me submit that no matter the hatred we extend to each other rather than love each other unconditionally, world peace is within reach. Let the diplomacy and stricter sanctions President Obama uses as magic wands prevail. If you want to catch a monkey, act like one without sniffing any rear ends. Leave that to monkey kingdom protocol to "be fruitful and multiply", unless you believe the evolution theory which tries to fool me that I once looked and acted like Chimps. Gash! That's it for me to push the red world war button right there.

I don't know about you, but I declare a feeling of higher level of safety and security during the first term of President Obama's tenure as the Commander-In-Chief. All I needed to stop being scared, living in fear on a daily basis watching over my back or shoulders, was to see on Television, the NAVY SEALS' dynamic and brave actions in that dreadful looking Pakistanis compound. Taking out the world's number one notorious terrorist, especially without a single loss of worthy life, as opposed to worthless, dangerous and world's nightmare of a human hater Osama Bin Laden, gave me hope that I may live to see my grand children graduate from college at least. Sweat dreams right?

That Commander-In-Chief's executive order, without typical consultation with Allied Partner Forces or even closest advisers that fameless night for OBL, which could have possibly let the cat out of the bag, making the job well done on Osama Bin Laden a nightmare for the Pakistani Immigrants around that compound, was a unique quality of an atypical world's most powerful leader, President of the United States of America, Barack Hussein Obama. I could not believe how fast the so called fiasco died down, considering the extent of the havocs plagued on humanity around the world by OBL. Too bad he was fed to some marine delicacies human beings could probably end up eating.

The existence of recorded threats which still shake the stability of world peace, like North Korea's stubborn and arrogant display of lavish military expenditure, testing and lunching nuclear war heads in vain, instead of feeding her malnutrition and starving people. Iran's confrontational pursuits similar nuclear arm race, camouflaged by statement of enrichment to bolster power needs. Both threaten world peace. I can say that Barack Obama as a Senator fiercely objected the Iraq invasion. My God, if fate did not make him the 44th. President of the United States if America, who knows how many more lives of able Americans and innocent Iraqis, would be sorrowful in our minds and of the whole world by now? That would be the answer to why a man threw a stinking shoe at the then most powerful man on earth.

I wonder why it's taking the world so long to put into perspective, a particular religion and its worshipers or followers, who support and continue to cause havoc around the world. Terrorism against a nation which predominantly professed "In God We Trust" through Jesus Christ is a human defect of the being and antagonizes God intention for creation. Putting it into perspective is as in finding ways, or influential persons like Barack Obama, whose childhood religious background confirmed he was exposed to Islam, but later in adult life, proclaimed Christian religion as his intended root to salvation and his achieved status as an American President to engage in International dialogue with fellow world Immigrants and try to forge world peace, such as typical United Nations establishment. We ought to take the spirit of Soccer World Cup or Summer Olympic Games as example, when the Opening and Closing Ceremonies often highlight human crave for World Peace.

Unlike the majority of people or precisely Presidents around the world, Barack Obama is blessed with sacred spiritual and natural attributes he can and already using to forge world peace. I have mentioned his dual religious ascriptions, which provide him avenue to communicate freely with both Islamic and Christian religions, rather than the usual Christian hypocrisy which turns off the Islamic world and ignites deepest human anger.

For peace sake, I think people should stop the hypocritical insult of Islam, Muslims, Quran and Prophet Mohammed. If such annoying gestures are directed to other religions especially Christianity, we condemn them as sacrilegious blasphemy, especially when our Savior Jesus Christ, the Holy Bible or the Cross is insulted. Does it occur to any Christian that some believers who worship God via other religious orthodoxy really view our bowing down to the cross as worshiping a wooden, metal or any other substance we used in creating the cross, as idol worshiping?

The world peace I think would cap Obama's ultimate goal for humanity is hindered when orthodoxy of one's religion is classified unspiritual, ungodly, artificial or lacking a Savior by orthodoxy of another religion. I contend that racism is not as volatile to 3rd. world war as much as the disrespect amongst religious epithets verbally, literarily or in any other way, catapulted between believers and worshipers of different religions. The whole world Immigrants as in all human beings on planet earth, need to practice acceptance, tolerance and endurance of each other's differences and let world Immigrants exercise modus vivendi between religions of our epoch, until the God we all worship comes bye to judge the quick and the dead. Opposite must attract for love and peace to prevail.

The history behind Halloween is very scary. It is the reason most horrible artifacts on Halloween night of October 31st. forget Friday the 13th., which America enjoys her capitalistic killer instinct represent. Scary is understatement when you read that some human beings out of the context of their creation and only because different tones of PEACH colors, often just killed other human beings by hanging them on trees with ropes. Unlike capital punishment ordered on notorious criminals for horrendous crimes against humanity. Lynching as it is popularly known, also has a type of three similar letter stigmas as we think of the devil's number 666. These three alphabets are KKK.

Stop right here to ponder my thinking. Considering you are a real proud and patriotic American who loves this beautiful land and knows that you are a descendant of an American Immigrant, imagine that you are at an International competition of patriots of several nations or countries for humanistic empowerment conference, vying for the most outstanding humanitarian deed Award, usually presented to a contestant or representative who has contributed for the betterment of humanity in their respective countries. Awards like Nobel Prize for humanitarian deeds. As an American, you are applauded for positive Human Rights activities, philanthropic gestures like "Secret Millionaires", Good Samaritan deeds by American Red Cross and a host of other Christian Missionary projects around the world. In the audience, a dark skin teenager rose up and shouted, "You killed my father by hanging him to a tree with a rope while you wore a white hood to cover your face". I don't know if shame is adequate to express what I would feel, but I sure will shed some painful and rueful tears to beg for forgiveness of such crime against humanity we put each other through because of different hues of peach skin colors.

How does all these exposition relate to someone I believe is a possible world peace pioneer? Fate has those three KKK alphabets ascribed to Barack Hussein Obama by nature. He is far from being a perfect human being as I didn't like he was a tobacco fume chimney, but stands a chance to tell the world that anger due to racism is supposed to be history not to be forgotten, but can be forgiven.

Speaking of human imperfections, even though the Holy Bible says we are all created in God's image or likeness, but gruesome acts of hatred between God's creations because of difference in skin colors, I see is a betrayal of the most human imperfection anyone can execute. No human being is perfect, but instigating or acting angrily towards a fellow earthly Immigrant is extreme transparency in betraying imperfection of inhumane trait.

I don't know of any human being that can claim authority to change the negativity associated with the stigmatic letters KKK, by imploring forgiveness for that aspect of ugly American cultural history of lynching one human being by another than President Barack Obama. I want to submit that the world has forgiven America's white hooded and slave masters' crimes of the past. I hope you got it right. I wrote forgiven as I have, but not forgotten, especially by some hard heads I hope this book will lighten the darkness of their hearts in the name of world peace as we are all related. Go get a peach and find your skin color on it. You will learn to forgive.

These three remarkable attributes of being a multi-religiously enthroned, interracially affluent and empathetically and spiritually KKK forgiven uniquely bestowed on him, make President Barack Obama atypical humankind en route to carving world peace for all Earthly Immigrants.

I don't know about you, but since the NAVY SEALS did away with Osama Bin Laden, I sort of stop looking over my shoulder in fear. As long as we all listen, follow and adhere to some instructions portray by a TV ad, which warns us to "say something" when you see a suspicious luggage or package on a train, bus or airport, we will be more safe for a long time to come. This Osama Bin Laden thing tops my Commander-In-Chief's job well done.

I noticed that when our brave men and women in uniforms were withdrawn from unnecessary invasion of Iraq, news about Iraq was no more in conflict with my cup of tea on a daily basis. More so are Al Qaeda atrocious activities which are obviously showing decline because Mr. Osama Bin Laden became history to have visited this world, I started sleeping more peacefully, but with my doors still bolted tightly in two places and always switched on my imaginary electrocuting device on my wired yard fence to deter uninvited guests on my property especially at night.

At times, I still wonder how much longer it's taking the world to put into perspective, the sickening evidences associated with blood baths, the believers of a supposedly peaceful religion created by another human being just born like you and I, go all over the world terrorizing mankind with spilling innocent peoples' blood. I respect my fellow human beings; I just can't seem to comprehend a religious orthodoxy, which supports suicide bombings. My heart tells me my assumption may be wrong because Islam is portrayed as a peaceful religion by my Muslim pals, but its still mind bungling to accept Al Qaeda groups claiming responsibilities for such atrocities of September 11, 2001, or of PAN AM explosion and numerous suicide bombings around the world by Islamist Extremists.

I submit that if human beings have breath of life associated with God who created the world in five days and man in His likeness on the sixth day, we must be somewhat spiritual. Remember the Angelic and spiritual intussusception of our Lord and Savior Jesus Christ, via the womb of unblemished Virgin Mary, and throughout His embryogenic incubation, is the spirituality that sustains Christian religion by faith till today. To some, I think that faith is an unbearable burden on will power. It makes it very difficult for some of our Earthly Immigrants to latch on to faith in Jesus Christ and thus rely on so many unspiritual doctrines. Thereby distracting and distancing them from connecting with God's unconditional love, which is the main missing ingredient in peaceful world recipe. My Gash! I wish God did not expel that Satan into the world He created for us all. Adam and Eve wouldn't have sinned, eating the forbidden fruit. Can you imaging what the world Immigrants could say to Tina Turner, singing "What's Love got to do with it", if we all could just meander around the Garden of Eden in our birthday suits, being fruitful and multiplying without prejudice against different shades of human skin colors? The world would be so peaceful, unlike later on after Moses brought the two tablets of the Ten Commandments and made incest immoral. Says who? I don't think God meant it to be. Do you?

Lets all go back in time to the Garden of Eden. No TV, no space station, no satanic snake and definitely no nuclear arms race. Just Beyonce and JayZ, Mariah Carry and her twin children's father, Justin Bieber and Selena Gomez I pray, or another lucky Commoner, which Prince Harry can't wait to honor with HRM the Duchess of Canterbury, possibly from Jamaica too? My goodness! His grandmother would love world peace gesture that far fetched. I also wish John F. Kennedy Jr. and Lady Klein especially was not taken away from us so abruptly too. "Be fruitful and multiply" would be the least blessings God would bestow on us through Adam and Eve. Those pair alone who in the Garden of Eden had "33 sons and 23 daughters" (5), could have been doing that without the curse to sweat on Adam and the pain to bear the Human fruits on Eve. The point here is that if we are made to think that we are all related through Adam and Eve, I submit that we probably will not hate each other to extreme of lynching one another because of different skin pigments. Obama's multi-racial blessing is showing the world that human being can be harmoniously beautiful and eternally peaceful with each other en masse.

Though exposed to Islamic rituals as a young lad, Barack Hussein Obama declares his religious affiliation to Christianity. He was married in a Christian atmosphere to a lady I think is earthly 'Rock of Gibraltar' of his strength, who not only comforts him to handle being the most powerful worker in the world. Understanding that the First Lady Michelle Obama was Barack Obama's Boss at a law firm, makes me think that the world is yet to taste the capacity with which Barack Obama's atypical presidency is forging world peace out of unconditional God's love. He must be honored with a second term to solidify what American Presidents should be doing to continue forging world peace. After all, beside Adam and Eve in the Garden of Eden, the whole wide world is borne out of massive immigrations.

I was at a wedding of my dear and respected friends Ronnie and 'Lady Di' as I love to refer to her because of her gracefulness. They were my co-workers at Bausch and Lomb contact Lens manufacturing Company in Rochester, New York. At one point, the DJ at the wedding asked the groom to stretch out his right hand with the palm facing downwards and then asked the bride to stretch out her hand out, open and facing upwards under the groom's hand. Then the DJ Said "Ronnie, this is the last time you will be the boss on top in the house. Of course Lady Di exclaimed that he is the head of her love life thenceforth. That added to many loving speeches that witnessed many tearful but deeply joyful faces of expression of passionate love between the Mr. Romeo Fabio, Ebony looking groom and Ivory Cinderella of Juliet statuesque bride's families.

Oh! It was very beautiful, how they both manifest God's wishes for mankind to love and comfort each other, irrespective of which color tone of the peach fruit, with which God blessed each and every one of us.

Jesus Christ came in the likeness of mankind, even though unbelievably spiritual, physically lived just 33 years, performed miraculous healing wonders that no other spirit filled human being to my knowledge could or would ever match, no matter the diabolic advancement in technology or science. Go ahead and keep cloning mankind for cell harvest, history will never be the same, compared to the spirituality with which humankind is composed. I am not aware of any other religion boasting of a Savior, who appealed to God as His Father to forgive us that we know not what we did to Him. The moment Judas Iscariot betrayed Him, up to His crucifixion on the cross, from where he bled precious blood for our salvation, I can't imagine when people say they don't believe in God, but "Oh God"—not George Burns the Actor please. Respect is not for sale. Fortunately to know God is alive in people's hearts even if they rebel against Him, that "Oh God!" is the first exclamation in pain that comes from their buccal cavities, when in accidents or just hitting their toes on stuck pebble, tree or root studs for walking clumsily.

(5) Jewish historian Josephus—
http://www.answersingenesis.org/articles/nab/who-was-cains-wife

CHAPTER 5

Second Term I Pray, solidifies "Change! Yes We Can" with "Audacity of Hope"

Since President Obama is now viewed as a Christian by majority of World Immigrants, I think he is in good hands for a second term. He is cool, calm and collected, especially under intense antagonisms. Just like Christian missionaries I have known since age 6, 7, or 8, when I lived with my dearest Great Aunt Mrs. Mary Odumosu, "Ye Bosen" as my beloved grand mother used to call her daughter. She manifested unparalleled caliber of an educator prowess at the United Missionary College, where future Teachers undergo pupilages tutelary in Ibadan of Oyo State in Nigeria, West Africa. A very light skinned Nun,—I am trying to refrain from negative figure of speech as in referring to another human being like myself as White—lifted me on her lap for a send off group picture with other Student Teachers many years ago. Ever since, I have rummaged my three brains as to why only few people in that area at that time were so light skinned, compared to my chestnut tone. Auntie told me that they were Catholic Christian Nuns bringing healing and peaceful words of God through Christ to our nation. Without the words of God through Christ, I see President Obama as peaceful ambassador to the world. Particularly as he conjures both Muslim credential when he was young and a Christian baptismal certificate my guess and now, he in a position as the most powerful man in the world, that is waving the flag of world peace, appealing to all earthly Immigrants to echo "All we are saying, give peace a chance" by one nation to another nation around the four corners of the earth or across the globe. GIVE PEACE A CHANCE.

Sitting on her lap for the group photograph is an understatement of pride and joy to be so close to a much lighter skin color world Immigrant like me, compared to my deep feelings of immense comfort and caring with which the Catholic Christian Nuns operated on a daily basis. They spoke very softly and mildly, walk with such peaceful gestures and spoiled me rotten with exotic imported cookies and candies which to this day, I refuse to erase from my memory.

I think that President Obama chose Christianity when he became an adult over the Islamic orthodox he was being modeled when he was under the authority of his Muslim stepfather in Indonesia, because peacekeeper attribute is ascribed to him by his spirituality and by birth.

Ever wonder why it did not matter, until it was time for him as a Commander-In-Chief of the most powerful nation I think is the capital of the world, to start ripping the benefits of being dually religions savvy. Which I submit is a political tool, he is ironically using to shed lights into the darkness of our Immigrant stubborn but world peace craving hearts in silence to start thinking world peace. Conflicts between these two religions from time immemorial, has been the number one major world problem that have claimed millions of lives, making attainment of a peaceful world something like imaginary illusion beyond our reach.

I submit that some United States of America's Immigrants in general, do not realize how naturally and spiritually diversified and politically toned atypical this first, multi racial—mulatto, Commander-In-Chief, Barack Hussein Obama really is as The President of the United States of America. If like me you didn't know him as much as I know about him to write this book, check record archive. He has another inspirational and motivational book out titled "AUDACITY OF HOPE". Maybe it will help you stop backbiting, stop doubting his birth certificate Dear Mr. Casino with due respect, stop condemning him for his dual religious connections and definitely stop being guilty of negative use of color blind figure of speech, calling him black and white together. Go back to kindergarten to refresh your color wheel 101 syllabus which tells you that black and white are no colors but only used to tone primary, secondary and millions of colors derived from mixing those colors together.

Knowing President Barack Hussein Obama during his first term alone has given me some classic characteristics to look for in candidates for US Presidency, when voting for future American Presidents. President Obama has established attributable qualities to look for, which I believe will at least include connotative omens, contingent possible avenue for people around the world and in particular America, omens suggestive of peaceful human gestures such as, stop being disrespectful, stop creating alienation referring to fellow human beings as white or black objects or plain arrogance to belittle other world Immigrants like yourself. In exhibiting such detrimental attitude towards each other, we are dishonoring God's magnificent artworks in molding each and every one of us in His own image.

In considering President Obama for a second term, get a hold of an Internet article by Rick Jervis of USA TODAY dated June 3, 2012. "From New Orleans—It's unanimous: A panel of renowned astrologers predicted President Obama will win re-election in November" The United Astrology Conference meets every four years—hmm! Like the Summer Olympics—and is the largest gathering of astrologers from around the globe and for the first time, this year's conference included contingent from China. Highlight of each conference is the presidential prediction. At the last conference, in May 2008, six panelists unanimously predicted Obama's win over Senator John McCain. Speaking reverently about a political rookie.

In my Pentecostal faith, sooth saying, card and tarot readings for fortunetelling etc, I am weary of, but ancient and present astrological readings of the future and especially the weather forecasters of today's technological marvels, invoke some curiosities in someone like me. By the way, don't forget that I changed from supporting Hillary Clinton to support Obama because of three peacekeeper attributes I believe President Obama is spiritually and naturally ascribed and achieved, to possibly help forge world peace.

The world is at the observation podium with snake eyes binoculars, in preparation to catch any voting irregularities that the astrologers also warned about. They cautioned that Mercury retrograde-an alignment of Mercury, the sun and earth—begins on Election Day and could lead to voting irregularities. Last time Mercury retrograde appeared on Election Day was on November 7, 2000 when it took a Florida recount and Supreme Court decision to finally, but regrettably put America on a 4-year $480 Billions extravagant pursuit of bogus WEAPONS OF MASS DESTRUCTION in Iraq. Knowing how politically toned President Obama is, cum all astrological wind vanes and majority Democratic paper windmills pointing index fingers to his re-election, I doubt if the world will give preference to the maxim of chameleon Déjà vu this November. I think voting for someone, who looks like typical warmonger from whom character assassination without merit flies uncontrollably, would further drive possible world peace to Hades.

What in the world could be more insulting or really provoking when someone who says he has the interest of Americans at heart, refers to Russia as America's #1 foe? I thought anyone my age would at least leave the Cold war race alone. Just like President Reagan said, "Tear the wall down", so I say let the sleeping dog lay down quietly, unless you have some stinking fleshes you want cleaned from your bones. "Yo-ho" my earthly Immigrant brother over there across the miles and oceans, I am enjoying your cool, keep keeping it calm. Thank you so much. Obama and Putin look like brothers. So I hope.

When it comes to things about the first Atypical American President Barack Hussein Obama, making election voting hanky panky not so easy for CHEATERS in America is now iron clasped protocol. Any right thinking faculty should think twice before trying to pull such ridiculous crime of "take a trick or treat" Halloween joke. It's not a laughing matter any more. Leave that to Eric Holden Attorney General's domain. I could hear him singing his version of my Country Music legend Willie Nelson's lyrics thus 'No more "on the road again" but we will get to the Promised Land' and "To a Maximum Correctional Facility without possible parole and don't dream of appeal, hereby banned for life." And bang goes the gavel.

America strives on DEMOCRACY and the rest of the world is just beginning to learn and appreciate the beauty and true context of "We the People, by the people, for the people" is all about. Ergo, we intend to keep it immaculately snow white quality clean this November endlessly.

CHAPTER 6

Whole World future Immigrants deserve a shot at world peace

I wanted to suggest a change or rephrase the adage which insinuates "do unto others as you would want done unto you", to 'do to others as done to you', by making immigration a norm with which world Immigrants would identify as part of being a human being on earth. This will enlighten people that being an Immigrant as we all are in America, would soften or make people think twice of the opportunity they enjoy as Immigrants, before inconsiderately bullying other people to return to wherever they departed. Only if such people knew their roots whence to America. I got goose pumped, thinking of crimes against humanity might become epidemic. Ergo, I am not starting any war. However, "As you lay your bed, so you'll lie on it" comes to mind when thinking of my two AfricAsiAmerican Musketeers "Royal Oaths", Eunice and Michael III. To tell you that there are any 24/7 since they were ejaculated as full-grown embryos, I did not ponder their life expectancies becoming abrupt because of Peace-less world dangerous acts, would be a transparent and extremely bogus lie.

I seldom read or watch NEWSPAPER or Television reports until it is the weather forecast time. I must always prepare myself to combat all the commotion involved in worldly exhibition of my Ceramic Art Works on the WWW. This involves what I want to accomplish the next day of my professionalism, especially when I live in Santa Clause region of the world, where the sight of snow flakes make us give thanks to my Creator and my Lord and Savior Jesus Christ. Getting exposed to frozen finger bitten experience would definitely bring the best out of

Samson or Goliath. No need for Samson's wife to shave his dreadlocks that robbed him of his strength or pebble from David's slinger that made the Philistine Goliath a stool to the Israelites feet.

How could innocent people on that 9/11 terrorist acts, know they were being flown to collide with buildings for most horrifying atrocity to watch on TV news? May God grant them everlasting peaceful rest? Can humanity justify numerous unprovoked shootings of innocent school children, religious worshippers or suicide bombers? Even natural disasters we bring upon ourselves warming up the atmosphere are not close to 'the world is coming to an end' predictions. I don't think so. Do you?

When you cut trees that absorb heat ray or wave from the Sun and industrialize the region with fumes producing technology, thereby polluting the air we breathe, we are practicing July forth barbecuing of ourselves. Don't forget life endangerment, dumping contaminants into rivers, seas or mighty oceans. So many countless ways we inconvenient the self and make us prone to peace-less world, fighting each other for the right of wrong with which we confront each other on a daily basis, world peace will always elude us indefinitely.

What can make fellow world Immigrants prioritize the fight for world peace a prima facie concern? Let Spike Lee, Steven Spielberg and the likes of movie directors and producers storm the world with childbirth PG rated movies. What am I saying? I mean for all audiences since

Elementary grade school pupils are already being taught puberty topics, and let all of us with parental company where necessary, witness the birth of embryos. Hear the baby's first cry for attention or first step of the baby. Or the first word mamma-ma or papa-pa of the baby and remind them of those sleepless nights because the baby is restless. How about Gabby D's and her Medallist Uncle Michael Phelps personal sacrifices to win Gold Medals at the London 2012 Olympics? Could it be Mamoud Ahmadinejad of Iran or the young North Korean 'Head of State', flexing nuke muscles, causing vehement irregular vibrations of pink organs behind the sternums in human beings around the world?

Back to the basics of dumb figurative speech we use to refer to each other as black or white. Lack of courage to forgive but not forget, so negative history is put at bay from recurrence. Could it be our total distancing of ourselves from the infinite God who created the world peacefully for 5 days, man in His own image the sixth day and tried to show us how to enjoy His peaceful creation by resting on the seventh day? No wonder we try to emulate taking vacation on cruise ships and sipping those margaritas and rum raisin ice cream for desert. Wow! World Immigrants, you came a long way en route to luxurious civilization. Got any more room on the next vacation Shuttle to Mars? Did I just read that you can tell your Automobile your next destination without touching the steering wheel, while your pair of pants is having problems staying up in the back seat with Kunfu Kid hitch hiking? Lord, have mercy. Immigrants are worse than Monkeys' recitations of their multiplication homework projects.

Whatever, we need to realize that our passage on earth is not ad-infinitum classified. Unlike Adam who lived 930 years having 33 boys and 23 daughters who all committed incest to populate the earth as He blessed them "Be fruitful and multiply". Could it be the latest Guinness Book of World Record report of the death of oldest human of less than 120 years, which reminds me that we are reducing fast in human being life span on earth? OH thou WORLD PEACE, your majestic arrival long over due since yesteryears or 100 of years ago. Try Y2K, when Christian Pastors preached that Jesus Christ alleged He would return.

All I am trying to get across is the need to start thinking that WORLD PEACE is necessary for royal oaths yet to be intussuscepted for embryogenic incubated fermentation for future harvesting, to make the world endless and affirm God's blessings of "Be fruitful and multiply" to hold its grounds. The seven firmaments will open and PEACE will drop on us "as gentle rain from heaven."

I can't comprehend how many glorifying praises future World Immigrants would accord the past world inhabitants, if some peace is attained and people live as God wished for us in the Garden of Eden. Maybe not as primitive as when the earth was created, but I suspect less sophisticated crimes will be in-existence or mild today.

The Commander-In-Chief President Barack Hussein Obama comes to play in this chapter because of the three attributes bestowed on him spiritually and naturally, which the world needs to think positive that world peace is within human reach.

A wonderful peaceful scenario will be the PLO declaring Israel a friendly neighbor. Gesturing the sharing of Ramadan feast with her in the name of PEACE God wishes on us all, and the Christians continue to share Christmas carols and some cookies and milk at the doorsteps of peaceful Muslims next door. I submit that the world's numerous sub major problems like starvation in some part of the world, battle against aids virus, President Reagan already caused Berlin wall to fall, disrespect and ethnocentrism, recession—where? Unemployment, dirty politics, college tuition skyrocketing through the chimneys, health Insurance back into California gold rush epoch and so many other uncertain future hindrances will become history. World's loving people enjoying and would do anything to keep peace permanent around the world, would work amicably to make the world a better place and avoid extra celestial flying saucer invasions. The Vault of the seven firmaments will create embouchures for the quality of mercy, like the gentle rain from Heaven to fall on peaceful Earth and all her Immigrants will live happily ever after.

CHAPTER 7

World Peace Treaty

Every human being ought to sign and subscribe to it

Irrespective of individual stand on any issue affecting the populace, a President when sworn into Office, subscribed to some kind of obligatory swooning oath, to protect all groups' interests indiscriminately. Example is Obama as the President, far from being Gay; he has Michelle, Marla and Sasha as evidence, yet he did not authoritatively condemn those who find it comforting to capitalize on their human rights and practice Adam and Adam or Eve and Eve duel under the sheet or which ever way they chose to express affection for each other.

Even though I'd rather reinforce what God's exotic sensuality for mankind to multiply the earth is, when He created Eve using Adam's rib to comfort him breaking his rib-poor Adam. Wow! How kind God is ha! Attacking gay rights in any way is against the opportunity that could broker world peace people. We should just think they rather be sinless like Pope Benedict and his priests and Nuns, who choose not to commit incest like the rest of the world is doing, whooping up storms down memory lane of sacred vows at the Alter, ". . . to comfort each other, for the richer or poorer, in sickness or in good health" indiscriminately, and especially with our extended Immigrants around the world, pretending we are not related as civilization mandates.

We are all started by Adam and Eve as stated from the beginning of the Bible Genesis 1:1 all through Revelation 22:21. Unless you are hiding any book that states God created Jorge and Blush or other human beings in another Garden of Love somewhere else on Waikiki beach in

Hawaii USA. Ergo, with whom or where did Cain, Seth—Abel already murdered—and other brothers, 32 in all with which Eve swamped Adam also 23 daughters, started populating the Earth you must ask. Don't look at me, I can pretend to be as naïve as you are if you claim not to know, but I believe that the Bible has the answer. Writing this book makes the third time I read the whole book of the Bible and still come short if God created any other human being which He breathed the breath of life into. He who is tired of learning is not fit to leave. Please help the rest of the world on that topic if you can, so we can justify our guilty conscience against incest.

My son's Grade 5 Teacher Mr. Fagans believes in repetition as it reinforces remembrance. It worked because my son was unfairly delayed in Kindergarten much earlier in his educational exploration. The school thought he had speech problem, disregarding my concern that he was mixing his bilingual Mandarin Taiwanese language with we 'gonna,' we 'wonna' and 'whatchumacallit' rhetoric, but often came home with honor role placements. 'Darn it' says the ancient Queen of England. Except that we grabbed our Independence by force, she must be tweeting from her grave onto Internet via FACEBOOK, lamenting Royal Navy's UN-NAVY SEAL'S elite military prowess, letting America loose from the bondage chains of colonialism on July 4$^{th.}$ 1776.

Should you wonder, the above is to justify the following repetition of the Bible verses I already capitalized on earlier? So bear with me or do what you must with the book. No apologies pal. Look at who is craving WORLD PEACE. Watch it dude and damsels. I heard that Kris Rock, Lady Gaga ET Queen Latifah.

Here we go. Ready, set. Go.

Out of all the countless books in this world on creation, the Bible, Authorized King James Version, is the first literature, which narrates to me in Genesis Chapter 1 verse 1, started with "In the beginning God created the heaven and the earth." It continues to confirm all the other things He created every day. On the sixth day according to verse 26, God said, "Let us make man in our image, after our likeness. I wonder with whom He was talking the storm, like a University Professor demonstrating and explaining project in progress to students in attendance.

In Chapter 27, "God created man in his *own* image, in the image of God created he him; male and female created he them." Think about that for a moment. Like a Sculptor, God created just one handsome male called Adam from sand, after which He breathed life into it, transforming it into a soulful human being. God then used one of Adam's ribs to model just one beautiful female I didn't get to meet, but looking at Halle Berry or Linda Carter with watery mouth, God's creation must have been a knock out dead gorgeous. After all, God only creates damsels we drool all over ourselves, just thinking of them how much more meeting them. However God named His own creation Eve and then blessed her and Adam to be "fruitful and multiply". And so they deed in deed, boasting 33 sons and

23 cutie pies and I submit that they wore different skin pigments too.

At one point I called one of my Christian Ministers Pastor Bishop Samuel Salyer in Ohio, to confirm that God did not create any other Human being besides Adam and Eve. From "In the beginning . . ." as in Gen. 1:1 until the last verse of the last book of the Bible as in Revelation, Chapter 22 verse 21 which ends thus, "The grace of our Lord Jesus Christ be with you all. Amen". In my High School, Bible Knowledge is the only subject I got Grade A in my WAEC = West African Examination Council which is like American GED final examination. Ergo, I conclude that there is no where in the entire Bible, or maybe any other religious book in which I could read that God Almighty physically created any other human being in His likeness. Also confirmed in Genesis 2:20 that Adam gave names to all the cattle, to all fowl of the air and to every beast of the field; but for Adam there was not found any match maker that could help him find a suitable partner, until God hypnotized him into a deep romantic somber dream of Eve as the Lord made him one from one of his ribs.

Learned Evolutionists try to confuse me with their theories that human beings who were created in the likeness of God were like Apes or Gorillas at one point. That we once crawled on 4 hinges and gradually walked on two feet. I wish Air Jordan is till sweating it out with the Chicago "BULL" and would slam-dunk that theory once and for all till eternity. I still confront their theories with us human beings, irrespective of the endless pigments of our peripheral complexions and even though science of Biology shows my vertebral column ends in shape of a tail, I hold fast with iron clad that we are all distant generations of our first parent Ancestral Immigrants—Adam and Eve. It is thus blasphemous and totally sacrilegious to liken God's creation in His likeness to Apes and Gorillas. Ergo, where did the notion of Apelike humans or when did God's created human beings become furry Apes and Gorillas? No Artist's rendition, neither Atheism doctrine which rejects the existence of God, nor Deist who thinks God is not interested in what He created, would penetrate the thick Christian skin by which I am covered with faith. Omnipotence and omnipresence are evidenced in everything that breaths air and react to photosynthesis of the Sun, which the Earth God created pays absolutely non-defying homage. No Evolutionist can scare me out of my pants with some fictional movie character of some hairy costume dude roaming the wilderness.

I often wonder about what was or were the religion(s) like before the birth of Jesus Christ. I am just glad that I was a spirit in heaven, waiting for God to bless my biological parents with a bouncing baby boy-me, who weighed close to 10 Lbs., when I made very loud triumphant entry onto Earth. Alas! She yelled. It's a boy! The native midwife in attendance exclaimed, gasping for air when God's curse on having babies was manifesting on my poor mother Florence. Born into a Christian family, which despite my mother being a product of Islamic father yoking with my Christian father, influenced my mother's Christianity conversion before and after I was born. That makes me share some similar birthrights with Marla and Sasha Obama who were born into Christianity genre to a father with Islamic traits in him. Wows wee! No wonder I feel compelled about this project on Obama's Presidency model. Talk about my homeboy connection. I am proud.

I praise God Almighty through our Lord and Savior Jesus Christ for being born into Christianity where "Love thy neighbor as thyself", is catechism defining pros and cons of Christian behaviors. I have not changed and continue to practice Christian orthodoxy and promise my Creator God Almighty not to change until I knock at Heaven's gate. Hopefully, I would have earned enough credits as a Christian to follow my Savior Jesus Christ through Heaven's gate, into God's Kingdom where I won't ever be hungry, thirsty or ever cry again. I hope you know that there is no gnashing of teeth but singing alleluia praise to God Almighty with the Angels wearing white flowing robes like the Angels. Not like the Klan's uniforms. You can now justify calling me a white man, cause I am now a spirit.

So why is religion a weapon of mass conviction of Immigrants towards attainment of world peace during Barack Hussein Obama's presidency model and thereafter? I know some of the ratio 1 voters against his ratio 2 voters' victory over Senator McCain in 2008 were not part of the victorious 2 millions plus. I am convinced that they did not understand that his Islamic background is a blessing in disguise. Now I hope you see how President Obama uses that long time ago connection to appeal to all religions in America. I contend that if it wasn't Barack Hussein

Obama in the action room when Osama Bin Laden was erased from the face of the earth, 9/11 or similar heartless Déjà vu could have taken place by now. All such or close attempts have been twitted to shame and OBL henchmen I believe are on the decrease and on the run, as we pray for the sake of world peace.

This is so emotional for me. I thought I have some really so called close Christian friends, who won't even take my telephone calls anymore because I campaigned and voted for a Democrat who they said is a Muslim, while others said he supports abortion. Now that he shows that a president is obliged to protect all Immigrants even if they are gay, and some smart Alex so to speak still doubt his citizenship, even after physical document of his Hawaiian birthplace, make me submit that hypocrisy is worst than incest. It won't be any wonder or I won't rule it out of stupidity that some would like to denounce Hawaii as a State in Unites States of America.

To shame some people, Barack Hussein Obama finally and authoritatively uses his mix color or universal complexion and dual religion citizenry as spiritual, natural and political weapons, to silence unwarranted stories about him and try to clean the world of her peace antagonists. He treads religious domains with authority and ironically brokers indirect peaceful dialogues with oppositions, which termed it siding with enemies. Not withstanding, he outcast's one Islamic Dictator one after the other across the miles from the Oval Office, without spending $10 Billions a month. Watch how the unrest in the Arab world is demarcating their region for peaceful transition from dictator rulers to Democratic Nations.

Now as some self proclaimed Christian whom I noticed stopped praying for their leaders as commanded by Jesus Christ they worship, Barack Hussein Obama wades his spiritual wands as the Commander-In-Chief from the Oval Office or Action Room from where he watches Obamaristic commands materialize. In such events like that which took out Libyan dictator Moammar Gadhafi or dethroned Hosni Mubarak of Egypt and especially the "Night Watch", not as in Rembrandt's painting but as in the elite NAVY SEAL'S diabolic military prowess in plucking out the world's number one Terrorist enemy Osama Bin Laden. Number 2 followed suit and so have all numbers 3, 4, and as much as haters of humanity refuse to let world peace take effect, they may continue to follow suite in the name of world peace. I pray that God will lighten the darkness of their hearts, so the whole world could start feeling world peace and safety in the horizon not too far in the distance for future Immigrants that will peacefully continue the nomadic culture of roaming the earth, confirming that human beings are world Immigrants wherever they habitate.

Upon all the threats, hatred, anger and animosities directed toward the United States of America, I submit spiritually that a hair can not and will not be permitted by invisible active force of God Almighty, be pulled against her sovereignty. Some religious people would say the sins are too heavy to warrant her destruction. God will declare that even though when sinners are punished for their iniquities and innocent people partake, the United States of America will not fall under any circumstance, except to give birth to world peace via democratic infiltration of world Governments abusing their citizens, with realistic utopian politics currently being modeled by President Barack Hussein Obama of the United States of America. A condition of world peace the whole world craves in silence because of fright imposed on human subjects around the world. But democracy will set free the oppressed.

America's supreme military power is a formidable fortress against any antagonist entity. Nonetheless, the fact that the United States of America is a melting pot of all kinds of Adam and Eve extended descending Immigrants, when her sinners are being punished will not be enough to affect all her other innocent Immigrants. Unfortunately, unbearable natural disasters are always finding ways to invoke our praising God endlessly.

President Barack Hussein Obama won by a ratio of 2-1 in the millions in 2008. The ratio of innocent Americans against her sinners is overwhelmingly higher now than then and the good Lord of heavenly host is thinking more than twice to destroy it. He would rather sustain it for the higher ratio of those who work relentlessly toward world peace, rather than those shedding innocent blood in unprovoked wars and terrorism out of unfounded anger and hatred because of religious and different complexion we ought to be thankful for around the globe.

America may be experiencing devastating natural disasters or heartless crimes against each other here and there and now and then, but I believe that God Almighty in all His merciful faithfulness, already promised not to destroy the earth with water again. Thinking of nuclear threats? I believe that through faith and prayers of innocent Immigrants which accounts for all of us, before a lunatic sinner or world peace hater pushes destructive button, God in His infinite power, is already scattering their angry thoughts, words and proposed deeds, to shameful threads under the canopy of cowardice.

One might ask about suicide bombers and gun wailing person against another person. Again, what better way can God punish sinners, if we can be brainwashed to die as sinners flying planes into buildings We will continue to pray for God's mercy to rain divine peace upon such souls.

Should you ever want to see, hear and especially feel and experience Pentecostal spiritual miracles of God through Jesus Christ the Savior, tune in to prayer warriors of The Holy Flock of Christ. Prayer conference line is 1-218-862-1300, enter the conference code 735061 on Sundays and Wednesdays at 9:30 PM EST and prepare to be spiritually touched and blessed according to the depth and strength of your faith in Jesus Christ, even via telephone lines.

President Barack Hussein Obama is a positive omen to America's Democracy and an illustrator of world leader that earns respect by giving respect. I propose that he is campaigning for world peace to start a treaty, which every Immigrant in the world should approve with selflessness to other people's needs and subscribe to its implementation around the world. He has spent his first term in the Oval Office by doing terrific job to better not only life in America, but also to show the world what kind of leaders we need to elect to serve us in a peaceful world.

To my fellow Americans:

WHAT TIME IS IT?

IS IT NOVEMBER 4 YET?

WHAT ARE YOU WAITING FOR TO BE A REGISTERED VOTER?

DO YOU WANT WORLD PEACE AND SAFETY OVER WARS AND THREATS?

DO YOU WANT AMERICAN JOBS BACK UNDER HOMELAND SECURITY PROTECTION?

I SURE HOPE YOU WANT HEALTH INSURANCE FOR ALL IMMIGRANT AMERICANS

Then work toward WORLD PEACE in your own little Immigrant status.

CHAPTER 8

Random Thoughts

My thoughts literarily orate that since the Earth is incomprehensively massive containing unbelievable countless human cultures cum many centuries gone bye to the delusion of mankind, the delusiveness in such minds have robbed our present generational Immigrants, the spiritual tenet of its creation by an invisible active force I perceive as God Almighty.

In this world and on this earth today, I tend to believe that we as her nomadic Immigrants at wherever situation we inhabit on the face of the planet earth, have created numerous religions from time immemorial and thereby have sowed seeds of strangeness that gave birth to alienation from God Almighty the Creator of heaven and earth and all that dwell in it and particularly from each other, out of which the end result is hate amongst ourselves, became customary norm in relating with one another.

Even though human beings naturally deliberate between what is wrong and what is right within themselves before acting either out, which in essence is the breath God exhaled into us through Adam his only physical creation besides Eve, I believe that some people still claim indifference to God as the creator of planet Earth. The spirit of God breathed into all of us at birth via Adam since the Garden of Eden, gave us free will to guide us in determining how we process the three significant routes of human gestures which are thoughts, words and deeds, for better manifestation of a positive or negative self to one another. The world will be a lot peaceful only if we listen to the spirit in each and every one of us which implores us spiritually to respect, honor, appreciate, adore and love each other peacefully without letting the silent voice in us be "gone with the wind".

Gone with the wind from the heart of some people are like those who grew up, learned and acquired so much knowledge and many things in life, only to fly planes carrying innocent people into standing buildings full of more innocent people on September 11, 2001, in New York State of America, is a saddest example of imperfection people whose Godly Spirit have gone with the wind display from their hearts.

I like to think of the magnitude of accomplishment it would be, if Barack Hussein Obama has been a Pastor like Billy Graham, but only preaching to the world that we are brothers and sisters, Aunties and Uncles, half cousins or distant relatives, mothers and fathers and grandparents from the same root to life, maybe my own tears I ended up eating with my breakfast on 9/11 2012 just watching people read names of loved ones perished on 9/11 eleven years earlier, especially hearing children read names and ended with "my father" or "my mother we miss you" would have been tears of joy for loving each other in a peaceful world, rather than painful tears of deep sorrow. Despite a fact I can say that the shame on humanity that infamous day of 9/11 did not affect me directly, unfortunately for me and millions of fellow Immigrants around the world, I was directly affected by the emotion and empathy that filled the earth on that day and on each of that day of 9/11 to come ad infinitum.

Listing President Barack Hussein Obama's first term accomplishments and achievements so far, I consider propaganda to give this book unnecessary volume. Nonetheless, from January 1, 2009 when Obama sat on the Commander-In-Chief chair in the Oval Office of the United States of America's White House for the first time, he and his administration have recorded several achievements and accomplishments one after the other almost every day of every month. On record under "Barack Obama Administration Accomplishments and Achievements List" are the unflinching tenets which show that beside March and November of 2009, November of 2010 and March, April, July, October and November of 2011, President Obama and his administration accomplished and achieved deeds to benefit Americans and humanity at large in all of the other months of the past 3 years and still counting in 2012. Besides those remarkable history making credits, I am convinced that the 2 million to 1 million ratio camping voters who put Barack Hussein Obama where God Almighty created him to pass through in his life's span, knew he is ascribed a peace keeper, even before he was awarded the prestigious Nobel peace price. Count how many Presidents around the world you know that won the Nobel Peace Price, especially less than a year in Office, I think you'd get an idea of why majority of well known world astrologers during their convention every 4 years, predicted in 2008 and again for his re-lection as the President in 2012.

On foreign politics as opposed to policies, we leave that to our ablest HLSS = Honorable Lady Secretary of State or HARM = Her American Royal Majesty, Madam Hilary Rodman Clinton with my utmost respect and admiration to be an outstanding Secretary of State you'd ever seen in action on world issues. Her unparalleled Secretary of State prowess around the world, paves way and provides President Obama the platform in which he sits on the Oval Office on Pennsylvania Avenue, hopefully sipping some green tea because I know he doesn't smoke any more, but authoritatively sweating it out, giving births to Democratic Governments around the world where human rights abuse is against God's blessing on Adam and Eve to multiply and be fruitful.

Like in Egypt and Libya that may look chaotic for the moment while the spiritual adage that when sinners are punished, innocent people partake takes it course, but will eventually be in line toward peace in the Middle East and other Arab Nations. Evidence which points that world peace based on mutual respect between religions is inevitable in the nearest future. He also sits in the operation room of his rented White House Mansion of 4 years, hopefully for another 4 more years of peace keeping process to materialize, and watches the most wanted human being on earth taken out, which may look bad or insolent to a Pakistanis, but peaceful to the world at large. He then picks up the red phone and tells Dictators across the miles, over deepest seas and mightiest oceans, to step down or face the mayhems of "CHANGE! YES WE CAN" after he gave those people abused by human rights criminals the ammunition they need which is loaded with 'AUDACITY OF HOPE". You see what happens within weeks or days, such Dictators became extinct or permanently sick and bed ridden who knows till their dying days. If for just all these "missions impossible" by the late enterprise of past Presidents for world peace, that President Obama could put in motion and without a single American's life or blood lost or shed through direct invasion or unprovoked wars, I must give Obama another 4 year shot at world peace and let him solidify what I believe God created and vested Barack Hussein Obama to bring into the world.

Let me remind you that this is just thinking out loud brain; you have till November 4 to join the real HOLY CRUSADE and make peace in the world a possibility by voting for the right candidate of peace. All I can reiterate to you and capitalize on is gut feelings and my spiritual Pentecostal belief that President Barack Obama has three spiritual and natural attributes God fated on him to help forge world peace by placing him in the White House. He is both Islamic atoned and Christianity redeemed, racially multi-blessed and out of the ordinary, he carries KKK stigma with a positive mind of forgiveness and implore the world to follow suit in forgiven each other of racism, slavery, holocaust, atrocious Jihad and all other crimes against humanity via power hungry unnecessary wars that have plagued the world from time immemorial. Peace is within reach if we so choose or majority of peaceful minded voters here in America and the whole world at large will mandate peace the world deserves. Don't miss the peaceful train.

President Barack Hussein Obama is a peaceful train, clunking peaceful engine on peaceful rail road around the world, which peace seems unbelievably illusive but in essence is in transformation stage. His birth is reminiscent of three supernatural problems that make life not so peaceful but make him a possible instrument of peace maker for the descendants of our first parents Adam and Eve. Hence, I submit that his birth is miraculously ascribed the three stigmata of human imperfection that make world peace an optical illusion and alluring imagination of a peaceful world, but ironically possible solutions to divine peace the world craves in silence. Is it a miracle that Obama is both Muslim and Christian by fate, do you doubt the miracle of his multi-racial existence and how come I see KKK written on his forehead, pleading on behalf of humanity for unconditional total forgiveness of human imperfections?

Miracle is superficial to humanity unless witnessed, relived by experience or by fate of faithfulness in those privileged with profound spiritual civility. Personally, my spirituality claim holds tight in miracles I have witnessed, experienced and lived through.

It's a miracle that a baby girl written off by medical profession of earthly Doctors who professed her not to live more than couple of days, confirmed that miraculous tenet of Jesus Christ's mission in life is a reality. For on the very first Wednesday her parents laid her down at Jesus Christ's feet on the cross via the Holy Flock of Christ prayer warriors, and they spiritually implored God's healing power with humble supplication through His Son Jesus Christ of Nazareth the Spiritual Healer, for His mercy to descend upon a child that could neither see nor move her limbs. Just as we finished praying for her and before the Pastor could say the final grace to end the prayer conference that night, the baby's father holding her in his hand—yes in one hand as tiny as she was described, shouted over the phone—get that and yes over the teleconference prayer line—saying "Pastor hold! Hold on!!" I did not doubt the Pastor's brave belief when he popped the spirit filled question "what is Grace's miracle?' Uche, the baby's father made a joyful exhalative proclamation of Grace's miracle saying "Grace just opened her eyes following the telephone handset trying to grab it from me. Pastor, I've heard of miracles but one is happening right here in my house". I wish Deists, nihilists, existentialists or any other atheist or polytheist indoctrinated persons were on the prayer line that evening to taste the sacred juice of the Holy Spirit of Jesus Christ at work or at least hear how believers in Jesus Christ by faith can praise Holy Trinity our God Almighty, when they shouted our popular phrase of "Alleluia praise the Lord", expressing joy and happiness in our Lord and giving Him all the glory.

Another miracle to the deepest of my heart involves my son Michael III the third. He was 12 days old when we rushed him into emergency room because of yellowish foam oozing out from his left eye. When the technician couldn't find his vein to draw blood and discovered that he had only 50% oxygen count instead of 98%, she beckoned Doctor Buzzard I believe, who exclaimed "Oh no, we are loosing him!, we are loosing him!!". Michael III then died for about 4 minutes on an examination table at Strong Memorial Hospital in Rochester, New York. His lips, eye lids and face all turned blue black. At that point, I yelled 'Spirit of the living God, let Thy presence be known right now.' Michael III moved, thrusting his chest up forcefully trying to inhale air. After an immediate balloon insertion to aide his breathing and an 8.5-hour open heart surgery operation on the third day at 15 days old, and a very hot water accident on his incision area at Rochester Chinese Christian Church barely a year after the operation, Michael III is 12 years old now with no side effect and zero restriction to his physical activities. I call him hamburger bouncer, capable of letting 3-5 hamburgers disappear with hot French fries in less than 10-15 minutes of purchase. Again praise God Almighty. Devil is a liar and made a big mistake coming to my house. Wish it thought of the meaning of my last name before attempting its foiled devilish mission, breaking people hearts in this world.

"Kukute o se mi, eni mi kukukte mi ra e pa." It implies that the root in the deep ground can not be moved, unless at the mover's defeat and succumbing to death.

Also, I somersaulted 4 times in a rented car on US 22 driving to Las Vegas in Nevada from St. George in

Utah where I won Bronze Medal in Chess Tournament at the Huntsman Senior World Games in 2008. When the automobile finally rested upside down, I could not reach to unbuckle my seat belt so I could crawl out. Not panicky at that point until I started smelling Gasoline and imagined the faces of my 2 AfricAsiAmerican Musketeers, both pleading with me "Daddy please get out". At that point, I calmly begged God to give me another lease on life to help Him raise the children He placed under my fatherhood to them.

Soonest I prayed that little but effective prayer, an Angel in form of a male stranger came out of nowhere, broke the driver side window, crawled in with my blood all over the roof now upside down, unbuckled my seat belt and pulled me out to safety. Less than 3 minutes after he pulled me out, the car exploded and started burning while the stranger pulled me further away from the inferno. I later looked around for the stranger to thank him but realized that he was also a God sent miracle. The guy was no where to be seen as I was being driven to the hospital in emergency vehicle.

Considering American history, it is a miracle that Barack Hussein Obama is the first dark skinned Immigrant on American soil to be the President of the United States of America. He is atypical U.S.A. Commander-In-Chief. Unlike all the past 43 typical American Presidents who have been all light skinned, President Obama is the first to be initially raised in both religions of Islam and Christianity, the two religions that is trying to end the existence of the world because of lack of respect to what they both hold sacred that their worshipers who believe in them could practice their orthodoxy to make the world a better place rather than antagonize each other to extinction. To me, it is also no wonder but a miracle that this same individual came out interracially blessed to show anyone who hates another human being because of God's blessings of various pigments of human skin colors, hates him or herself and needs total forgiveness of the self.

If the world Immigrants wherever we are, can and want to see these two human phenomenal omens as blessings rather than curses, the third detrimental phenomena of Lynching one another wouldn't have taken place if we realized we were killing our own brothers, sisters, mothers, fathers, children or grand parents, from distant relationships through Adam and Eve. America suffered that epidemic long time ago when brothers from the south fought their brothers from the north in a civil war. Lord is merciful.

President Barack Hussein Obama I submit that he is spiritually and naturally a political model on Democratic runway, on which his brave "Change! Yes We Can" appeal established a very difficult path for future American Presidential Politicians with any skeleton in the closet, would find it a formidable wall or mountain to scale over or tread without having characteristic grandiose of a peace maker and keeper, which could induce unity, respect, admiration, compassion, peace and the "greatest one is love" in voters and in all World Immigrants on planet earth.

DIVINE HOPE

I bid you farewell my brothers and sisters of the world and hope we all can repent to broker world peace with our creator God Almighty before we breathe our last breaths and head on to Heavens gate.

God grant all Immigrants on the planet Earth which He created for us, with His unconditional love, spiritual peace, divine and merciful blessings.

GOD SAVE AND BLESS AMERICA FOR US NOW AND ALL OUR FUTURE IMMIGRANTS, AS ORDERED BY THE CONSTITUTION OF THE UNITED STATES OF AMERICA

AMEN